GOING BACK

Gary McKay served in Viet Nam as a platoon commander and has been back to Viet Nam four times in the past ten years. He has written several books on the war, including *In Good Company*; *Delta Four*; *Bullets, Beans & Bandages*; *On Patrol with the SAS*; *All Guts and No Glory* (with Bob Buick); *Jungle Tracks* (with Graeme Nicholas); and *Viet Nam Shots* (with Elizabeth Stewart). He is a full-time non-fiction writer and freelance historian.

GARY McKAY

GOING BACK

Australian veterans return to Viet Nam

ALLEN&UNWIN

First published in 2007

Allen & Unwin
83 Alexander Street
Crows Nest NSW 2065
Australia
Phone: (61 2) 8425 0100
Fax: (61 2) 9906 2218
Email: info@allenandunwin.com
Web: www.allenandunwin.com

National Library of Australia
Cataloguing-in-Publication entry:

   Going back : Australian veterans return to Viet Nam.

   Bibliography.
   Includes index.
   ISBN 978 1 74114 634 9 (pbk.)

   1. Vietnam War, 1961–1975 – Veterans – Australia. 2.
   Veterans – Travel – Vietnam. 3. Vietnam War, 1961–1975 –
   Personal narratives, Australian. 4. Vietnam – Description
   and travel. I. Title.

959.7043394

Set in 11.5/15 pt Requiem by Midland Typesetters, Australia
Printed in Australia by McPherson's Printing Group

10 9 8 7 6 5 4 3 2 1

CONTENTS

FOREWORD
Going back, gaining closure

Dare it be written that never, in the field of bringing closure to the personal equation of human conflict, has so much been done for so many by just one: namely Gary McKay as author of this book. With apologies to Winston Churchill, I have amended his famous Battle of Britain declaration to salute a most vital effect of this book, which provides many examples of the bittersweet experience of veterans returning to the very ground where they lost their legs or their mates or both.

The Viet Nam War was, in many ways, a young person's war on all sides, in part because the National Service call-up in Australia reduced the average age of soldiers in combat to around twenty-one. In turn this has meant these veterans, post the Viet Nam War, have some fifty years or more to live, and so a long time to dwell on their memories of Viet Nam and all the agonies encountered there.

Matching this in recent times is a huge upswing in the affordability of overseas travel: as Viet Nam opened up its tourist industry many veterans became curious to return and, after a taste of modern Viet Nam and after overcoming any personal demons, they have kept on returning.

However, not all have had the time, desire or wherewithal to visit; for those veterans, this book offers the next best thing: a set of epic accounts of veterans 'going back' to read and be enriched by. Equally, those about to go back can prepare a whole lot better for that return visit by absorbing the good, the bad and the ugly that may be encountered.

Above all else, this book will help many to gain an enhanced sense of closure, something that was never going to be easy given the way the war ended for the allies. The defeat was not so much at the hands of the North Vietnamese but at the hands of the Pentagon and various US Defense Secretaries and other strategists, who made big mistakes and allowed the war to continue even after they had recognised they were on the wrong track.

As Gary McKay writes, no Australian who served in Viet Nam has anything to be ashamed of, but the losses remain a big cross to bear, including those veterans who made it safely back but then died prematurely due to post traumatic stress disorder and other ills.

The Vietnamese also sustained huge losses in this curious war and will write the war their way. But bit by bit the rhetoric moves towards the immortal words of Kemal Atatürk, then addressed to the mothers of Anzac soldiers, embracing and saluting their contribution at Gallipoli: 'After having lost their lives on this land, they have become our sons as well.'

Gaining closure will be greatly helped by this book, a long overdue and necessary postscript to the Viet Nam War (or American War or, more accurately, the Pentagon War).

Tim Fischer
Ex 1 RAR and former Deputy Prime Minister

Phuoc Tuy Province (c. 1965–75)

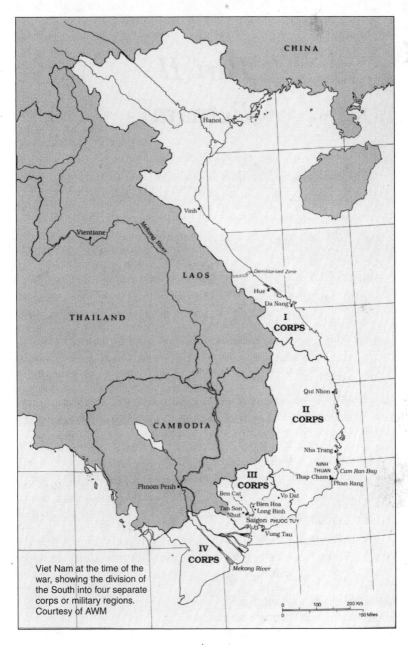

CHINA

Hanoi

Vinh

Vientiane

Mekong River

LAOS

THAILAND

Demilitarised Zone

Hue
Da Nang

I
CORPS

Qui Nhon

II
CORPS

CAMBODIA

Nha Trang

NINH
THUAN   Cam Ran Bay
Thap Cham
Phan Rang

III
CORPS

Phnom Penh

Ben Cat   Vo Dat
Tan Son   Bien Hoa
Nhut   Long Binh
Saigon PHUOC TUY
Vung Tau

IV
CORPS

Viet Nam at the time of the
war, showing the division of
the South into four separate
corps or military regions.
Courtesy of AWM

Mekong River

0   100   200 Km
0   150 Miles

PREFACE

As a young man I served in South Viet Nam in 1971 as a rifle platoon commander with the 4th Battalion of the Royal Australian Regiment (4 RAR). In 1993 I made my first trip back to Viet Nam because I was writing a book that was partly funded by a John Treloar Research Grant from the Australian War Memorial. I wanted to return to where I had served, fought and nearly died after being severely wounded. I saw very little of Viet Nam when I was first there at 23 years of age. All I had briefly seen was the port of Vung Tau, the 1st Australian Task Force (1 ATF) base of Nui Dat, and a very large number of trees and bushes as I patrolled through the tropical jungles of Phuoc Tuy Province.

Indeed, the first time I saw Tan Son Nhut airport in Ho Chi Minh City was in late 1993, when 23 former members of Delta Company, 4 RAR, and a few ex-soldiers from 3 RAR and a sprinkling of wives landed for a three-week visit. It was stinking hot, extremely humid and had the rotting-vegetable smell of the tropics—just as the town of Vung Tau had smelt when I went there on a rest and con-valescence (R&C) break two decades before. Many other memories came flooding back almost straightaway, and I was constantly bombarded by flashbacks and recall of times good and bad, funny and sad.

I have since been back another five times, and always on a research trip of some description. With each new visit I have expanded my trips and taken in more of that beautiful country. In 2002 my 21-year-old daughter Kelly joined me on one such sojourn. She also fell in love with Viet Nam.

I realised that as Viet Nam veterans are approaching retirement and their kids are off their hands and their responsibilities have waned, many are now taking to the highways as 'grey nomads' and discovering Australia's beauty, or are taking off overseas. The number that are returning to Viet Nam for holidays and pilgrimages is growing, and I wanted to write this book to help other veterans decide whether to revisit the land where they served our nation in conflict, or whether perhaps to stay at home and buy the Winnebago instead.

To document the memories of those who have already made the journey back to Viet Nam, I gathered first-hand accounts from the men and their partners through interviews and letters, and I am indebted to them for allowing me to intrude into their private thoughts and recollections in compiling this book. I strongly suggest that those contemplating returning to their old battlefields grab a copy of my book *Australia's Battlefields in Viet Nam* for guidance; it also contains some suggested itineraries for those wanting to visit the Task Force area of operations. I also recommend that travellers obtain a copy of the latest edition of the Lonely Planet guide to Vietnam; it is well worth the money and has some very useful tips.

At times in this book I have used the term 'the American War'. The Second Indochina War (or Viet Nam

War, as the west referred to it) began after the Viet Nam Communist Party decided early in 1959 to sanction greater reliance on military activity and to start infiltrating South Viet Nam. Inside Viet Nam this war became known as the American War.

I am indebted to my publisher Ian Bowring of Allen & Unwin for allowing this little book to proceed. It is a niche book, but as befits Australia's Publisher of The Year for at least seven years, they do publish 'books that matter'. My thanks also go to my editors Clara Finlay and Katri Hilden, and to the 5 RAR tour group of 2005 who allowed me to accompany them to Viet Nam as a case study for this book. Their assistance, forgiveness and friendship are truly appreciated.

INTRODUCTION

For many veterans returning to Viet Nam, the visit will partly be a pilgrimage—a trip that will see them return to a place where normality was subsumed by abnormality, and where killing fellow human beings was tragically taken as the norm. A co-author of mine, Elizabeth Stewart, a historian at the Australian War Memorial, wrote a paper on pilgrimages and I am indebted to her for allowing me to quote extensively from her very well researched work. On the subject of pilgrimages she wrote:

> Pilgrimage: the Macquarie Dictionary definition describes it as a journey, especially a long one, made to some sacred place as an act of devotion. In the past, pilgrimage has been most often associated with religious customs and travel. Today, though, pilgrimage is increasingly associated with secular events. Think of the crowds that flock to Gracelands on the anniversary of the death of Elvis Presley, of the survivors and relatives and friends of those who died in the Bali bombings who congregate on Kuta Beach every year, and of course, the thousands of people who make the journey to Anzac Cove in Turkey every Anzac Day. Although many of the ceremonies held at these places have some religious content, they are largely

held to commemorate loss and offer a chance for public bereavement.[1]

For Viet Nam veterans, there are no national or state Viet Nam War cemeteries like we see at Gallipoli, on the Western Front in France, or in New Guinea. Those who died in Viet Nam were initially buried in the Australian section of the British War Cemetery at Terendak in Western Malaysia. This practice followed the Australian Government's longstanding policy of interring war dead only in cemeteries overseas. The policy was changed in 1966 after several Training Team members killed in action were brought home to Australia to be buried, their passage paid for by both American and Australian advisers.[2]

War historian Elizabeth Stewart suggests 'two types of people have traditionally made battlefields visits—the pilgrim, and the tourist'.

Tours to battlefields often contain a mix of both. The tourist is there out of interest; perhaps keen to make a family connection with a particular gravesite, or to see the places they have heard so much about. The pilgrim is a different kind of tourist. He or she is often a veteran or a relative of one, undertaking a mission which aims to help heal emotional wounds, or to pay tribute to fallen comrades. Members of a pilgrimage are a group with a united purpose—they want to revisit the past, learn more about themselves and gain a greater understanding of their war experience. Not all are searching for closure or resolution— some may be going out of interest to see old battle sites, and to once again enjoy the mateship that they experienced at the time of their war service. There is no one overriding reason why people undertake these journeys. To try and seek a simple explanation for them may indeed ascribe false motives to groups or individuals. To say that all Viet Nam veterans return to Viet Nam for closure on their wartime experience is too simple an explanation. Having said that, there is no doubt that for many of those who participate there is often a sense of anticipation and even fear beforehand, with a build-up to an often cathartic commemorative event during the tour, followed by a defined sense of relief and happiness. Pilgrims return home, richer for having undertaken the visit, and still closely bonded with those with whom they shared the experience.[3]

Prime Minister Robert Menzies committed Australian troops to the Second Indochina War on 25 April 1965. On 29 April he announced the deployment of a battalion of soldiers from 1 RAR to South Viet Nam, to help what he claimed was the struggle against incursions by the Communist north. Although initially widely approved by the Australian public, the Viet Nam conflict became Australia's longest military commitment, and the most divisive social issue of a generation.[4]

When Australian servicemen returned from South Viet Nam, they were sometimes accorded a parade through the streets of some of Australia's major cities, and occasionally regional centres such as Townsville in north Queensland, where a large military garrison was billeted. However, these were not celebratory homecoming parades of the sort

Australians witnessed at the end of the Second World War.
A few parades were marred by demonstrators, but overall
there was precious little recognition for the Viet Nam
veteran. What also differentiated the Viet Nam veteran
from other returned servicemen and women was that there
was no overall victory, no important military success to
celebrate: the fact that Australian units were never defeated
on the field of battle meant little in a war that was eventually abandoned and ultimately lost to the Communist cause.

As Elizabeth Stewart so perceptively noted:

> When Viet Nam veterans returned home to either apathy
> or outright hostility, many chose to remain silent, burying
> their wartime memories for many years. Most got on with
> their lives—married and worked, some with more success
> than others. Viet Nam memories were only revived occa-
> sionally—at Anzac Day reunions, or local unit gatherings,
> and shared only with those who had the same experiences
> to remember.[5]

In October 1987, Viet Nam veterans were given a Welcome
Home Parade in Sydney, and thousands turned out to cheer
on the men and women who had served their country
either as Regular or National Servicemen. But as many
veterans cynically observed, 'it was only fifteen years too
late'. On the fifth anniversary of the Welcome Home
Parade in 1992, a National Memorial was unveiled in
Canberra's Anzac Parade, the avenue leading up to the
Australian War Memorial, and veterans finally had a place
of homage on Australian soil where they could gather and
reflect as the occasion arose.

However, for many veterans the draw of Viet Nam remains powerful, and often conflicted. Issues of recognition, 'guilt' and involvement in an unpopular war all invite doubt and questioning: should they go back, or shouldn't they? Hopefully this book will help answer these questions.

—⚒—

In Viet Nam itself, the one constant is change. Very little has stayed the same, especially in the southern regions, which have witnessed spectacular economic development in the last few decades. When peace finally came to Viet Nam in 1975, the population was approximately 40 million. By 2006 it had more than doubled. Economically, growth in gross domestic product averaged 6.8 per cent per year from 1997 to 2004, despite the Asian financial crisis and a global recession, and hit 8 per cent in 2005, when it was estimated at US$235.2 billion. Meeting the demands of a booming population, of which a quarter are under the age of fourteen, has required massive change to cater for infrastructure and industrial growth, and membership in the ASEAN Free Trade Area and the US–Vietnam Bilateral Trade Agreement have precipitated even greater changes in the country's trade and economy.[6] The place is on the move.

As a result, much of what existed in the 1970s has been upgraded, or demolished and replaced by something more modern and twice the size, or subsumed by other development. For example, the macadam road between Vung Tau township and the provincial capital of Ba Ria (Phuoc Le) was a two-lane road that wound its way up the Vung Tau peninsula through small villages that specialised in producing *nuoc nam* (fish sauce) and left an indelible olfactory memory on the senses. Today that road is a four-lane kerbed and guttered tollway.

In the 1990s, increasing numbers of tour operators responded to the opening up of Viet Nam. They organised tours solely for tourists, but a growing part of their market was war veterans and their families. One veteran who began as a tourist but ended up running highly successful battlefield tours there was Garry Adams, who had served with 6 RAR in 1969–70. Towards the end of his tour of duty, he recalled sitting aboard an Iroquois, flying back to base, enjoying the view below of jungle, paddy fields and distant hills draped with mist. He thought then that it would be a good place to visit after the war. In 1994 he again saw the Viet Nam coastline from the air, this time on a flight from Singapore to Hong Kong. As he glimpsed the familiar ground below he felt he had to return, and did so in 1996. Dissatisfied with his first trip back, which he thought would give him closure on his war service, Garry returned again to Viet Nam with a tour company that he later joined, and has been taking veterans back to their battle sites ever since.[7]

Garry has some thoughtful insights into why Viet Nam veterans are returning in increasing numbers. Tourism has improved enormously, and many veterans have reached a point in their lives where they are financially able and emotionally ready to deal with their Viet Nam memories by confronting them head-on. While the dominant reason veterans return is for closure, many want to again experience the close mateship they shared during their tour of duty by returning with a group of veterans from the same unit. Their families are pilgrims too: many have lived with their father's or husband's Viet Nam experiences in one form or another, and want to see for themselves the places they have heard about. As well, they want to support the veteran as he confronts his memories, and gain a better understanding of what he went through so many years ago.[8]

—∿—

Pilgrimages to Viet Nam usually take a similar form. Most veterans are keen to see their former areas of operations, and most visits begin in Ho Chi Minh City (or Saigon, as veterans still refer to the former capital of South Viet Nam). On landing at Tan Son Nhut airport, the busiest airfield in the world during the war, many veterans are surprised to see so few relics of the war. This is to be a common theme of their visit. In Ho Chi Minh City, they visit various sites including the former Presidential Palace (now the Reunification Palace), and the markets of Cholon. Most tour groups then head into the former Australian area of operations, basing themselves in the coastal town of Vung Tau, formerly the location of the Australian logistics support base. Visits out of Vung Tau take in the towns of Ba Ria and Hoa Long, the Long Hai Hills—still a heavily mined and dangerous place—and, of course, the Long Tan Memorial Cross.[9]

This book looks at the sites that most Australian veterans will want to visit, including the base at Nui Dat, the logistic support base and town in Vung Tau, the

Horseshoe feature, the Long Tan Cross and areas such as the Long Hais, the Hat Dich area and towns like Binh Ba, Xuyen Moc and Ba Ria. The 5 RAR first tour veterans who made a pilgrimage in 2005 tailored their tour to take in specific locations that were important to them such as their lines in Nui Dat, the Long Hai Hills, the village of An Nhut and Long Son Island. For many veterans, simply driving the major arterials gives them the memory freshener they have been craving.

For a soldier, sailor or airman, returning to a battlefield is a very personal confrontation. War is one of the most life-changing events an individual could ever experience, and it shapes their personality, their behaviour and the way they live their lives. For many who have been involved in war—and not just the combatants—it is a time when they have their morals, beliefs and ideologies seriously challenged. Regardless of who they are, their family background and their education and social status, war affects them all—albeit to varying degrees.

As a veteran who has returned to my own battlefield many times, I decided the best way to write this book was to lay out all the facts and let veterans decide for themselves whether and how to undertake their own pilgrimage. This book concentrates on the areas in Viet Nam where most Australian forces served, Phuoc Tuy Province (now called Ba Ria–Vung Tau Province). To adequately cover the regions where the Australian Army Training Team Vietnam (AATTV) served would take another volume. For those readers wishing to gain a better idea I recommend the book *The Men Who Persevered*.[10]

For many Viet Nam War veterans the thought—and the practicalities—of going back where they served as soldiers, sailors and airmen is fraught with problems. For some it is the fact that they are now in their sixties and their health is beginning to falter, or even downright fail. For others it is not so much a physical or medical issue that concerns them but the thought of unlocking potential demons from the recesses of their mind.

I found myself in a similar situation back in 1993 when I was researching a book called *Delta Four—Australian Riflemen in Vietnam*.[II] I wanted to get a better grasp of the province in which I had fought, and also to interview the former enemy to discover their impressions and recollections of fighting against the Australians. I was distinctly nervous about the idea, especially as I was still serving in the Australian Regular Army as a lieutenant colonel. My fears were realised when it was discovered during my three-week visit that our tour party was being 'shadowed' as we travelled around Ho Chi Minh City, Vung Tau and around the old Phuoc Tuy Province. The 'agents' tracking our group were far from covert and were in fact captured on home video.

Thankfully that xenophobic approach to serving Australian Defence Force members has changed somewhat with the more 'open door' policy taken by the Vietnamese government, although serving personnel do attract some special attention at Customs and Immigration on arrival at Tan Son Nhut airport even today. However, the veteran who has no ties to today's military has nothing to worry about, and will pass through the airport much like the thousands of other foreign tourists flocking to the country every other day.

For veterans who were physically or emotionally scarred during their tour of duty, it is easy to understand any reluctance to revisit the country in which they were injured. The manner in which veterans recall the past can also have a bearing on how they approach the idea of returning to the war zone. For some it will simply be too painful to even contemplate. Others will want to return out of curiosity, or perhaps take a holiday in Asia and combine it with a visit to their 'old stamping ground'.

So when should one venture back? Most veterans are now in their late fifties or early sixties and consideration should be given to the extreme tropical conditions they will encounter. I asked Garry Adams, a veteran of some 40 tours, the best time of year to return and he replied:

> I think the best time is from August to October. Other than that I would say February or March. You could get into April or May when it is good; it is very dry so you haven't got to worry about wet weather or problems with getting into any of the places, but the heat tends to get to some people. Once you get here and get going it is okay, but initially it is very hot. Up in Hanoi you can get temperatures like 40 degrees [Celsius], and I have been here at Marble Mountain [Da Nang] when it has been 46 degrees [Celsius].[12]

Touring can be done with a group or individually, but as I hope to demonstrate by the end of this book, it is probably best done with someone accompanying the veteran, and for the first visit organised tour groups are probably the best way to go.

Not everyone who returns finds it a totally enjoyable experience, and a few even suffer flashbacks and post-tour problems—but in my experience, for the majority of veterans it is an experience they are glad they undertook. This book will not gloss over any difficulties that the veteran may encounter, but will try to present the situation in an unbiased and informative manner that will allow veterans to make a balanced decision on what avenues they wish to take.

Part I

THE VETERANS

Chapter 1

GREAT EXPECTATIONS

When deciding whether to return to Viet Nam, the veteran will be wondering what they are letting themselves in for. What will it be like? How much will things have changed? Will I be able to recognise anything? How will I respond if someone asks me if I was a soldier in Viet Nam during the war?

To help answer some of these questions, this book records the thoughts and experiences of those who have already been back.

I have accompanied five tour groups to Viet Nam and have observed a variety of pre-tour perceptions by veterans of what revisiting the war zone will be like, ranging from no preconceptions whatsoever to real concern that they will not be able to 'hold it together' when they return to where their mates were killed or wounded. My personal experience was something of an emotional rollercoaster, from being fascinated on the one hand by the progress of the country since 1975, to feelings of utter sadness when I stood where I had once helped load a dying soldier onto a Stokes litter for casualty evacuation, only to lose him in-flight. But such emotions are normal and natural, and should be expected—not something to be feared.

So what can one expect when returning to the place that marked, for most veterans, a watershed in their young lives? The responses to that question during the interviews in this book are as varied as the veterans themselves. Garry Adams was a Regular soldier, a corporal and infantryman serving with 6 RAR on its second tour of duty in 1969–70. Garry said he found his first visit 'very daunting':

> I was quite ill before I left, I had had my blood pressure checked and it had skyrocketed to 200 and something, and it was ridiculous. I was almost at the point where I wasn't going to come. But then after a while everything settled down and I was okay; once I got into the country I was all right and I didn't have any great problems at all.[1]

Garry is now a tour guide and tour director for Battle Tours, a company that specialises in taking veterans and their families back to battlefields.

Another former member of 6 RAR who served as a National Serviceman in South Viet Nam was Steve Campling. Steve had deployed to Viet Nam in 1969 as a reinforcement soldier before ending up in 6 RAR. Steve and his wife Gail both believed that the war was a waste of lives and effort, but wanted to see the country as it is today. Steve looked back to a tour he and Gail did with Garry in 2002 and recalled that he felt 'some trepidation at first, however as the tour started in Hanoi, I treated it the same as the many other tours I had done in South-East Asian countries and enjoyed the tourist experience'.[2]

From November 1969 to April 1970 Sergeant Derrill De Heer worked in the Operations Section of the battalion headquarters of 8 RAR churning out typewritten orders on Gestetner wax skins. Then he was posted to the formation of a new unit, the 1st Australian Psychological Operations Unit (1 Psyops Unit). He believed he got the job because he had 'previously served in Asian countries [Malaya and Thailand], was infantry, and intelligence-operator and signaller-trained'.[3] Derrill did a second tour in South Viet Nam with 4 RAR/NZ (Anzac) Battalion as the unit Intelligence Sergeant. Like many other veterans he thought the fall of South Viet Nam in 1975 was 'an absolute tragedy', adding Australia and the Allies 'let the South Vietnamese down' when the South finally succumbed to the Communists: 'I believe that the politicians in conjunction with the Americans sold them out.' His passion for Viet Nam has continued through his military and now academic career. Derrill went back to Viet Nam and the old Phuoc Tuy Province on a private trip in 2003:

> I wanted to show my wife where I had been, show her the beautiful places and the beautiful friendly people. We then went on an organised trip throughout Viet Nam and Cambodia. We just loved it. I went back again in 2005 for study purposes; again I loved the place. I would love to be able to help the people of the province, and I could easily live in Hanoi.[4]

Looking back

Staff Sergeant Bob Hann, who was the Company Quartermaster Sergeant with Delta Company, 4 RAR, in 1971–72, recalled how he felt when he left the country in March 1972. He was:

Glad to be going home to my family. I had no great feelings after the withdrawal because I felt that the lack of
resolve by the Americans in the final year or so made the
result inevitable. History will judge if the loss of 500-plus
of our prime young men was worth it.[5]

Another soldier who was with Bob Hann at the very end of
Australia's combat involvement in South Viet Nam was
mortarman Garry Heskett, who was attached to Delta
Company 4 RAR prior to the withdrawal of the battalion.
He recalled how he felt when he was leaving the country
after his tour of duty:

Being part of the last rifle company out of Viet Nam—
[leaving in] March 1972—I felt somewhat relieved I was
going home in one piece. However, I have never hidden
the fact that I felt cheated by a government that withdrew
us before the job was completed.[6]

When asked how he felt when the South fell, Garry
Heskett replied with a degree of sorrow:

I recall most vividly watching the fall of South Viet Nam
and Saigon on TV. I wept, feeling bitterness and anger
against the South Vietnamese for giving up the fight so
easy; anger at our government for not leaving us there
to protect and serve, making sure that there was proper
government infrastructure and defence capabilities in
place prior to departing; and sadness for our troops that
were killed or wounded.[7]

Garry's wife Suzanne accompanied him on their trip back
to Viet Nam in 1993 in an organised tour with a group of

fellow soldiers, mainly from 4 RAR's second tour of duty. Suzanne supported Australia's involvement in the war, coming, as she said, 'from a patriotic family' (her father had served in the Royal Australian Navy for six years in the 1950s). Suzanne admitted:

> I really didn't know what to expect; it wouldn't have been my choice for a holiday. However, I think it was important for me to go, as the place had had such a profound impact on Garry's life. I was hoping it would be helpful for him in a healing manner. It was also a way to picture in my mind this place called 'South Viet Nam'. I really was surprised to see such a 'rich-looking' place that at the same time was so utterly poor.[8]

National Serviceman Bill Kromwyk (pronounced 'Kromway') went to war in 1969 as an infantryman. He recalled how he felt when he was leaving South Viet Nam on a 'Freedom Bird' out of Tan Son Nhut after 12 months on active service:

> I was happy, I was glad to get out of the place. I felt I had had enough . . . Yes, [we were] just wasting our time and blokes were losing their arms and legs for nothing. Why do that? And we were causing so much upheaval in the country.[9]

Bill thought the collapse of South Viet Nam was inevitable and 'felt awful but not surprised'. He reflected on the position of the Army of the Republic of Viet Nam (ARVN) and the civilian populace who had supported the South Vietnamese governments:

I thought, well those poor bastards now. But I knew they didn't have the stamina to hold out. I just had that feeling; the North was more committed ... They would still be fighting today, if the Yanks hadn't pulled out and [the war] kept on going. They [the North] were never going to give up.[10]

Bill Kromwyk went back to Viet Nam in 2001 with a couple of close mates with whom he had served during the war, as he says, 'to see how the place looked after 30 years. What was it like there? Has much changed? And I guess we just wanted to go back to our old stamping grounds if you like.' This was a case of these blokes 'doing their own thing', although some very handy in-country contacts helped make their trip easier to arrange. Bill added:

We did our own individual visas through the travel agent and that went fairly smoothly. We decided we would start off in Hanoi and work our way south and exit from Ho Chi Minh City, and that is the way we did it. We went from Brisbane straight to Hanoi direct on Thai Airways— straight in—whack![11]

Peter Rogers was a second lieutenant pilot with 161 Recce Flight and saw out a tour of duty unscathed in 1969. He spent the bulk of his tour hovering over the lush green countryside trying to locate the enemy and occasionally getting shot at. When he left South Viet Nam he felt good:

I felt terrific; I was going home to a wife and a brand-new kid who was born during our tour. I was impressed with Qantas Airways who brought us home. Once we had got airborne they brought around ice cold bottles of full-cream milk. And everybody loved it because of the awful taste of that long-life stuff we used to have.[12]

When asked how he thought his tour of duty had gone Peter replied, 'Pretty good, yep. I had gone there for a purpose and it was the highlight of my Army career.' Like many young officers his tour carried with it a large amount of responsibility—and as a pilot it was even greater as decisions were based on information supplied by the Recce Flight. Peter Rogers was in Paris on holiday when he saw a newspaper shouting the news that the Communists had finally taken Saigon. He saw the banner headline and said, 'It really punched me in the guts. But we could see it coming from a long way off.' Peter returned to South Viet Nam in 2001 and 2003. On his first visit his wife of 40 years accompanied him; as Peter said, 'I wanted to show Suzie what it was like and I wanted to see the place again and see how it had changed.' Like Bill Kromwyk, Peter and Suzie Rogers organised their own trip:

> At the hotel we were staying at in Ho Chi Minh City we arranged for a car and driver for two days, and we stayed overnight in Vung Tau. The driver came along as an interpreter. It was great.[13]

But for his second trip back in 2003, Peter went on a 35-day trip with a tour group from the Sunshine Coast Vietnam Veterans Association. Peter described their marathon adventure:

> We started off in Hanoi, went down to Ha Long Bay, had an overnight on the boat, back to Hanoi and then went up

to Sapa and visited the Nung tribes people; that was interesting. They have a totally different culture and I thought
they were quite Mongolian, and I was very upset to learn
that the Vietnamese government keeps them on the outer.[14]

A tour of that magnitude would normally be very expensive, but one of the veterans owned a tour company and
was able to offset some overheads, as Peter explained:

The big thing about that trip was that we had our own bus
and we worked our way down the whole way by road, and
went to a lot of places the average person wouldn't see.
We stopped and ate at the local restaurants. It was great;
we met a lot of people. Went back to Ho Chi Minh City,
and then down to Phuoc Tuy, Vung Tau and Nui Dat, and
some went out to Long Tan. Then back to Saigon and then
down to the Delta. We also went out to the Cao Dai
temple [near Bien Hoa].[15]

What made it special for Peter's group also was that the
men already had a strong bond from their Association, and
many felt that the trip only strengthened those ties.

One man who showed a true sense of adventure on his
trip back in September 2004 was former gunner and
battery surveyor Ian Ryan. He arrived in South Viet Nam
in early January 1968 as a reinforcement with 106 Battery,
4 Field Regiment. His unit supported 7 RAR, but from the
end of April he worked with 102 Battery, 12 Field
Regiment supporting 1 RAR. Looking back on Australia's
involvement in the war, he reflected: 'In the end, I was saddened by the fact that there had been so much work put in

there without any positive outcome, only just a whole lot of pain and misery for many.'

Ian gave the background to why he returned to Viet Nam:

> I had been thinking of going back for some time, but it was after having been on the Kokoda Trail the year before that I became interested in returning to Viet Nam. I am involved in a church here in Melbourne and a group of us from Melbourne and Adelaide raised $12 500 to fit out a playroom and playground for a hospital that had been recently built in Tam Kay [70 kilometres south of Da Nang]. Before meeting up with them, I arrived on my own and spent three days touring around the old battle-fields and to the main Task Force base at Nui Dat, and the logistical support base at Vung Tau. I was going to hire a car and an interpreter, but instead was able to engage the services of a taxi driver in Saigon to take me to all the places I wanted to go to for the princely sum of $US200. Cheap at half the price! He was hopeless outside of Saigon. The bugger had absolutely no sense of direction.[16]

Mental and physical preparation

Apart from being medically fit to travel and fully inoculated, it is also important that veterans are mentally prepared for their return to the battlefield. In particular, they need to be aware that things have changed fairly dramatically, and sights and places that have been etched into memory will no longer look the same. As part of his preparation tour guide

Garry Adams contacts his tour group to set the scene for their visit:

> I speak with them on the phone and give them a brief outline of what the place is like now. I think it is important to let them know that it is quite safe to move around and they are not going to have people jumping out of the bushes at them with guns and all that sort of thing.[17]

Garry also ensures that the group acclimatises before reaching the battlefield areas, both physically and mentally:

> It sets their mind at rest . . . We always spend a few days in Saigon first to let them get back and to realise they are back in Viet Nam and it is not full of boogie men and they are not going to get shot at, and they are not going to get robbed—I mean they might get pick-pocketed if they are unlucky—but it eases them into it. And even if it is [only] two or three days it is always helpful to spend that time in Saigon first, or even in Hanoi if we are coming south. It just lets them get back into the swing of things, have a look at the city, and see how friendly the people are. Then we just take it from there step by step.[18]

But before even joining the group, the veteran must also be psychologically ready to tour. It is not in the best interests of the veteran or his family and friends if there are 'issues' that need to be resolved. As Garry Adams explains:

> I have had women ring up on behalf of their husband and say 'my husband needs to go back to Viet Nam because he has a lot of issues'. And I ask what issues does he have, and

they say, 'Oh, he beats me up and he beats the kids up and then runs out the back and hides behind the chook house, shouting out the VC are coming,' and all this sort of business. And 'he has been arrested for assaulting Asians down at the local supermarket'. I tell them, 'I can assure you he is not coming on our tour.'[19]

Thankfully those cases are very few. Most tour members are ready and more than willing to visit Viet Nam and immerse themselves back into the country.

However, it must be realised that Viet Nam is still a Third World nation, not a first-class tourist destination. There are no facilities for the disabled, and there is a distinct lack of public amenities away from the larger cities. It can be rough on the ladies at times, and carrying your own supplies is always strongly recommended.

Thoughts on the former enemy

Most tour groups will run into former South Vietnamese soldiers and may find the experience unsettling, as the men are now treated somewhat unfairly by the current political regime. Occasionally tour groups will also come into contact with former Viet Cong (VC) or North Vietnamese Army (NVA) soldiers, and this can be even more unsettling.

Men like Bob Hann had quite strong views on the former enemy. Bob returned to Viet Nam with me in 1993, and when asked if he ever felt sorry for them, replied, 'At the time never. After the trip back in 1993 I saw some things differently.'[20] Fellow infantryman Steve Campling expressed a similar sentiment when asked the same question: 'Never! It was them or me!' But that hasn't deterred Steve and his wife from returning for a second trip to Viet Nam, which they undertook in late 2006. For Steve events of war are now 'water under the bridge'.[21]

Derrill De Heer, who met and interviewed many prisoners and detainees during the war, had a different view of the former enemy:

> After many interviews and seeing the effects of abductions, kidnappings, assassinations and the destroying of government facilities used to achieve military and political ends, I'm not sorry for their leaders. I feel sorry and have a lot of sympathy for those who had been coerced into supporting the VC. I felt sorry for the peasants who lost limbs to the mines the VC placed where the locals were injured. I felt sorry for the people, as the VC [Communists] destroyed their society with fear, coercion, threats, kidnappings and assassinations, so they could build it in the way they wished.[22]

And that is one thing that may stick in the craw of some veterans: the manner in which the former enemy fought. It can be a sticking point to reconciling with the former foe— but only if the veteran allows it to be. I found it was easier to let bygones be bygones, and get on with living in the present. Many former enemy soldiers were only doing what they believed was right for their cause at the time.

Only rarely have I found that Australian servicemen actually 'hated' their enemy, and even then it was tempered with respect. Mortarman Garry Heskett viewed his former foe as 'a very resourceful and battle-hardened opponent which I hated on one hand, but respected on the other, for his skills in confrontation had been tested and honed over many years'.[23]

Ian Ryan saw the enemy uncomfortably close on a few occasions, especially at Fire Support Base Harrison during the Tet Offensive of 1968. As a gunner and battery surveyor he saw first hand how hot the action got as the enemy assaulted the Australian position. His view of them was pragmatic:

> At the time, I did not allow myself to think too much about them. Even when you saw their dead bodies, it had no impact on me whatsoever. The NVA I thought were very good soldiers and made the most of what little they had. I feel sure had they been better equipped and trained, who knows how much more damage they could have inflicted on the Allies. You have to remember that we were fighting on their terms and in areas that they knew well and they could easily blend in with the local population most of the time. I did, however, feel that they were expendable ('cannon fodder') by their leadership, and that how many of them would be killed in the process, it did not matter, as long as the end justified the means.[24]

Ian Ryan's supposition about the attitude of the enemy leaders is supported by Intelligence Sergeant Derrill De Heer, who had a great deal of contact with captured Viet Cong soldiers, and many others who had surrendered under the Chieu Hoi (surrender) program:

Many were uneducated, illiterate poor peasants. Some
had been abducted into the Viet Cong [units] and pressed
into service. The VC cadres were very good at indoctri-
nating these people. The VC volunteers who came back
under the 'returnee' program came back because they
were tired, hungry, needed medical treatment or had lost
the will to fight. After some time many of them didn't
believe their cadres anymore.[25]

Bill Kromwyk did his tour of duty as a machine-gunner
in the Tracker Platoon on 6 RAR's second tour of duty in
1969–70. His platoon had a 'successful' tour in that they
accounted for a number of enemy and lost no-one from
the Trackers. Bill offered these comments about the men
he fought against:

I suppose I did feel sorry [for them] a couple of times
after someone was shot. I remember one VC; his foot was
only just hanging on with a bit of tendon. He was being
lifted out by helicopter, and I can still see the look on his
face. He was in absolute agony. I suppose you feel a little
bit sorry there, but it could be you. I remember someone
throwing me the wallet from a dead Viet Cong soldier
and they said, 'Here Bill, that's yours.' Inside there were a
couple of family photos of his sisters and his mother, and
you don't feel good after that.[26]

Such moments of compassion were quite understandable,
although Bill also added that after a while he became 'a bit
hardened with them actually. But I was there to do a job
and I did it as best as I could.'[27]

Peter Rogers was attached to the Americans for a while on flying duties and was exposed to a different type of enemy, the NVA, that many in Phuoc Tuy Province didn't get to see too often. Peter described how he felt about them:

> When I was with the Americans we were up against the NVA almost exclusively. They were very well trained, well equipped and well disciplined. The local force—the VC— would pick up a rifle part-time and I don't think they had much idea of what was going on. The thing that got me was that they were fairly dedicated—very dedicated—and you had to have a lot of respect for them.[28]

No hard feelings

It is now 32 years since the war ended. Over the last two decades I have interviewed literally hundreds of Australian Viet Nam veterans. The common thread seems to be that the war was a dreadful waste of time, resources and lives— on both sides. But the veterans also realise that one cannot undo what has been done.

Many former Viet Cong that I have also spoken to on my six trips back to the Socialist Republic of Viet Nam state that they hold no grudge—indeed, many respected the Australian soldiers because they 'did not commit atrocities, took care of the Viet Cong wounded, buried their dead and tried to do something for the people of Phuoc Tuy Province'.[29]

In the fifteen years since I first returned to Viet Nam the attitude towards Australians who fought in the 'American War' has not changed: there is no animosity, anger or angst expressed towards the returning veteran. I have drunk beer and other potent substances (I am still not sure if it was avgas or alcohol) with our former enemy, and the stark realisation that we were all soldiers once—and young—is driven home most emphatically.

No-one has anything to be ashamed of, especially Australian veterans.

Chapter 2

THE 5 RAR TOUR GROUP

The 5th Battalion, RAR, replaced 1 RAR in Viet Nam in mid-1966 after being formed at Holsworthy outside Sydney a year before. They were the first infantry battalion to deploy overseas with conscripted National Servicemen. The 5th Battalion prepared for war by conducting platoon, then company and finally battalion exercises, and attended a battle efficiency course at the Jungle Training Centre in Canungra, Queensland, where they undertook the prescribed and predictable two weeks of scrub bashing. They were then engaged in, as former company commander, Major (later colonel) Paul Greenhalgh, described it, 'a wonderful training exercise at Gospers [north of Sydney] and conducted live firing exercises as well'.[1]

The battalion deployed primarily by air (via Manila), while one rifle company went by sea on the HMAS *Sydney*.[2] It was a unit of 'firsts', being the first infantry battalion to operate around Vung Tau on acclimatisation training, the first unit to move over the ground and secure the future Australian Task Force base at Nui Dat during Operation Hardihood, the first unit to occupy Nui Dat hill itself, and also suffered the first National Serviceman killed in action. Later, they would be the first unit to occupy The Horseshoe, south-west of Nui Dat.

The 5th Battalion was a very busy unit, with companies deploying on at least 26 operations during their tour of duty, meaning that of the 353 days in-country they spent 71 per cent of it on operations. On top of this heavy patrolling requirement, they also had to clear, secure and establish the Australian Task Force base from scratch. That meant days of digging, sandbagging, wiring and just clearing the bush in and around the disused rubber plantation. For the bulk of their tour they lived under hoochies and didn't have the luxury of the electricity, reticulated water and other facilities that later units enjoyed.

The modus operandi for 5 RAR and then 6 RAR in 1966–67 was to deploy to an area of operations and then patrol primarily on foot. Their aim was to search for and destroy the enemy who were operating in what was then called Phuoc Tuy Province. There was also a need to establish the Australian presence, which they achieved by conducting cordon and search operations that left the local populace in no doubt that there were new players in town.

The 5th Battalion has a very strong unit association. At a five-yearly reunion in Canberra in September 2005 it was estimated that some 900 former members attended. The idea of a pilgrimage for former officers was born some time between the laying up of the battalion's colours in April 2004 and the funeral of a former battalion chaplain in September 2004. It took about six months for Association President Roger Wainwright to sign up enough men to make the trip viable. He planned to return in October 2005 and by June of that year he had his group assembled.

These are the men who made up the 5 RAR tour group that returned to Viet Nam in 2005. Their ranks are given as they were in 1966.

Major Paul Greenhalgh, Officer Commanding Delta Company, 5 RAR

Paul was a Melbourne lad who decided to attend the Royal Military College (RMC) Duntroon in 1954. He graduated into the Infantry Corps as a lieutenant after four years. After an initial posting with a National Service battalion at Puckapunyal, he attended a parachute course and was then posted to 1 RAR, which was about to embark for service in Malaya in 1959. He served with 1 RAR as a rifle platoon commander with 7 Platoon, C Company, chasing Communist terrorists. As Paul commented, 'Without a doubt the greatest learning experience of anything was being a platoon commander in the jungles of Malaya, and believing you were going to catch Chin Peng.'[3] Paul then served with the SAS Company as a platoon commander, then as adjutant at RMC. He believed Malaya was a 'good training ground' for what he encountered in South Viet Nam in 1966, when he was posted on promotion to command Delta Company, 5 RAR.

Before deploying to Viet Nam, Paul arrived at Holsworthy, 'at the same time as about 70 per cent or 80 per cent of the company' and undertook an intense amount of training:

The structure of NCOs [non-commissioned officers] was there; the Regulars from the 1 RAR days and 5 RAR had only had about five or six months on its own anyhow. So it was an incredibly hectic time of training, which was planned very brilliantly by the CO [Commanding Officer] John Warr, by the senior staff at the battalion, and we just went hell for leather for five months before going away in May. It was just staggering what was done.[4]

Delta Company had a mixed bag of platoon commanders: Dennis Rainer (later to win a Military Cross), a Portsea graduate; Greg Negus, a full-time Citizen Military Forces (CMF) officer;[5] and Finnie Rowe, a senior graduate from the Officer Training Unit at Scheyville in the first intake of National Service.[6] Half of the soldiers were Regular Army; the remainder were National Servicemen serving out their two-year conscription—but they were all infantrymen trained under the same system. As Paul remarked, 'Obviously the older ones were Regulars but . . . there was no separation of class or anything at all, they were just all there together.'[7] By the time Major Greenhalgh deployed he had a good understanding of what the war in South Viet Nam was all about, adding that the unit they were to replace, 1 RAR, were preparing 5 RAR with training notes: 'We were definitely being fed the "dos and don'ts" and lessons learnt.'[8]

After securing the Nui Dat position through Operation Hardihood, it was six weeks before the Australian Task Force came in. As Paul stated, 'In a sense we were on our own and extremely vulnerable all that time.' When describing the nature of their operations he added:

The intensity was incredible and I don't know how that compared later on in battalions, but I would say being the first in there we were in the front line and vulnerable the whole damned time. At no stage did you feel that you could let your guard down, maybe down at Vung Tau when you were sitting on R&C when you got away from the place. But you seemed to have a 360-degree personal perimeter the whole time.[9]

Delta Company was spared mine incidents, but lost four killed in action in two separate incidents. Paul recalled, 'I remember having a service in the boozer on Nui Dat hill'. On discussing the enemy he faced, he thought their 'ability to fight was unquestioned . . . But right at the beginning I wondered about the Allies' ability to win this war.'[10] Primarily 5 RAR was continually running into local Viet Cong, and usually from D 445 *Provincial Mobile Force Battalion*.

Paul looks back on his tour of duty 'with incredible pride. My strongest legacy of the year in Viet Nam was the degree of professionalism that the soldiers attained, achieved—the National Servicemen particularly, because they were that youthful element.'[11] Paul missed out on a second tour of duty as a commanding officer but did command 5/7 RAR in December 1973. His reaction to the fall of South Viet Nam was one of 'shock and horror'. He remarked, 'I was at Canungra [instructing] on Tactics Wing and I remember about ten majors and myself listening to this announcement and saying, "Good God, all that effort has gone to waste." '[12]

Paul and his wife Wendy have been back to Viet Nam several times because their son has been living in Hanoi for eight years, running a motorbike touring company. When asked why he wanted to come on the 5 RAR pilgrimage, Paul replied:

> It's down memory lane to physically see the terrain of Viet Nam where we were. Maybe things have changed so much we won't see any comparison to what we had before. I have got photos; my son has actually been there twice and has been to Long Tan and all over the place. It is just down memory lane for a few days and to go with a few friends and to relive that time. To see Vung Tau, Cap St Jacques as it was, and of course we will end up seeing my son up in Hanoi.[13]

Initially Paul was totally against returning to Viet Nam, but after a battalion reunion in Wagga, NSW, a few years ago, and after the funeral of battalion chaplain Father John Williams in Sydney, he was convinced by fellow officer and Association President Roger Wainwright to take the journey back with a group of the battalion's first tour officers. He admitted he was 'just never really interested to come back to Viet Nam. It never really meant so much.' Even though Paul had been on many battle tours around the world, he said, 'For some reason I saw no need to come back here. But thank God I did.'[14]

Wife Wendy was delighted that Paul agreed to return with the 5 RAR group and was keen to accompany him because she wanted to see the country where he had fought. She had no expectations before the tour, adding, 'I wanted to see where he'd been to sort of fill in a jigsaw puzzle that wasn't quite complete.'[15]

Today Paul and Wendy live in busy retirement in Canberra, where Paul fills in his time as a top-notch picture framer.

Captain Ted Heffernan, RAAMC, Medical Officer, Nui Dat

Ted Heffernan is a large, stocky man with an infectious sense of humour. He became a doctor in the Royal Australian Army Medical Corps (RAAMC) after he had graduated from medical school via the Army's undergraduate program in 1964.[16] He served for five years in the Regular Army and in 1966 was posted to South Viet Nam as a regimental medical officer (RMO) in a field ambulance and in an artillery field regiment. He survived ambush and the other dangers of service in a war zone and returned to Australia after being decorated by the Government of South Viet Nam. Today, Dr Heffernan, FRACS, FRCS (England), FACS, is a general surgeon, and has a practice in Geelong, Victoria, where he lives with his wife Joy.

Ted wanted to return to Viet Nam to renew acquaintances, visit places where he deployed on Medcaps (medical civil aid programs) and share memories with his fellow officers:

It was probably the only chance I was going to get to get back to Viet Nam and see any of the spots I've served in with people of the same era, which is significant. And it probably wasn't a bad time in life. As you get older you haven't got much chance to do these things now.[17]

Ted's wife of 43 years wanted to return with him because 'it was a good time to come back with Ted and experience a number of places he's talked about for the last 40 years'. On reflection Joy added, 'I wanted to support him, and also to see the areas that Ted actually visited while he was in the Army here in 1966. And for myself to have some peace of mind.'[18]

Dr Heffernan treated Allies and enemy alike, and saw the physical and emotional damage that war can inflict on the human body and spirit. When he left South Viet Nam in 1967 he was 'pleased to leave unharmed'. He was dismayed at the result of the conflict, which carried a terrible loss of life on all sides, and deplored the withdrawal of the Allies in 1972, saying 'a core of loyal South Vietnamese were just left to their fate'.

Ted was unsure what he would see on his return to Viet Nam. 'I thought I would recognise nothing in our battlefields, and I didn't know how I'd feel about going to them.' But as he discovered later, 'there are certain landmarks that are still there. I think the best times for me on this trip were finding places like the RMO's tent in the field regiment and returning to Xuyen Moc and Hoa Long.' Joy also wasn't sure what to expect, remarking, 'I didn't expect it to be as pretty a country as it is. For some unknown reason I didn't expect it to be as green, quite as beautiful as I found it.'[19]

Ted is still practising surgery (to pay for Joy's extravagances, he says), while Joy undertakes retail therapy with relish.

Captain Peter Isaacs, Adjutant, 5 RAR

I first met Peter Isaacs—a captain instructor at the Officer Training Unit, Scheyville—in mid-1968 when I was an officer cadet. Peter fell into the stereotypical mould of the British Army officer, who spoke correctly, dressed immaculately and was never fazed. He wore a 'Herbie Johnson' forage cap with a steep visor that meant that you could never see where he was looking and if he was watching you. He taught infantry minor tactics and several other subjects and was regarded by most cadets I served with as a 'pretty good sort of bloke'. After serving as a platoon commander in the British Army in the United Kingdom, he joined the Australian Army on a five-year short-service commission and served with 5 RAR on its first tour of duty in 1966–67 as an intelligence officer and adjutant. For his service in South Viet Nam he was Mentioned in Despatches. After his time was up he returned to the United Kingdom and served with the Sultan of Oman's Armed Forces between 1975 and 1978 as a company commander and then battalion second-in-command on counter-insurgency operations in Dhofar Province. It was during this tour of duty in Oman that Peter was nearly killed in a landmine incident that took his right leg off at the hip, and severely chewed into his right arm and left leg. He also lost the sight in his left eye and was extremely lucky to survive.

Peter has been returning to Australia from the United Kingdom for decades to attend the five-year battalion reunions and events such as the Dedication of the Vietnam Memorial in Canberra in 1998. When asked why he travels halfway around the world to attend such events he simply replied, 'It's family. That's why.' Peter said he wanted to return to Viet Nam 'as a sort of "pilgrimage" to remember those fine young men with whom it was my privilege to serve in 5 RAR, and who did not return'.[20] His reservations were similar to those of many veterans who are contemplating a return visit:

> I had anticipated that much of the scenery would have changed—'development' in what used to be called the Third World usually means unplanned urban sprawl. I was not disappointed; travelling from Vung Tau to Ba Ria and Hoa Long is now a continual ribbon of buildings.[21]

This was to be Peter's first trip back to Viet Nam since the war. He expressed his expectations as being mainly:

> Comradeship—being among those men who I know better than any other group I have ever worked with— apart from another campaign I took part in, that is [Oman]. Thankfulness—to remember those fine fellows of our 5 RAR family who were killed in South Viet Nam.[22]

Peter was always frustrated in South Viet Nam because he felt that the Australian effort should have 'been more "belligerent"'. He favoured a more aggressive operational approach. When the South finally fell in 1975, Peter was heavily involved in operations in Oman. He described how he felt when he heard the news:

> I was involved in another war in '75; had little contact with the outside world and loving it. When I eventually

saw a film clip of the tank rolling into the Presidential
Palace, I was sad for the people we had tried to help, and
angry that public opinion in the US had brought about
the situation. Even more so when Henry Kissinger and his
North Vietnamese counterpart got the Nobel Peace
Prize![23]

Peter (married in 1964 but now divorced) was not in
favour of wives or partners being included in the trip, but
added ruefully: 'I realised it was inevitable (some would
not have been allowed to make the trip alone!).' It is testa-
ment to his grit and determination that he made the trip
because Viet Nam is not a country that caters well to
disabled people. However, he remarked that in his current
job with the United Nations managing landmine clearance
operations in Tajikistan he wasn't too worried about a
lack of facilities, and so he was sure he would manage 'just
fine'.[24]

Peter resides in England when not lifting mines in far-
flung outposts around the globe.

Lieutenant Ben Morris, Platoon Commander, 5 RAR, 2 RAR and 1 ATF Civil Affairs Detachment

Ben Morris graduated from RMC Duntroon in 1965 and
served initially with the 1st Battalion, Pacific Islands
Regiment (1 PIR), before being sent to South Viet Nam as a
reinforcement officer. He knew something of the war, having
received lectures from the staff and from Colonel Ted
Serong, who led the initial deployment of the Australian

Army Training Team Vietnam (AATTV). Another visiting lecturer in 1964 was Captain Peter Young, who Ben recalled 'giving us an extremely good briefing on Viet Nam'.[25]

Deploying as a reinforcement—commonly, but not disparagingly, referred to as a 'reo'—is probably the hardest and most demanding way to go to war. The reo often doesn't know the people he is about to serve and fight with, and he hasn't had the benefit of work-up training back in Australia where everyone becomes familiar with the standard operating procedures of the unit. Ben Morris described how he felt about his posting as a reinforcement officer:

> I wasn't happy about going to the Reinforcement Wing because I wanted to go and join a battalion ... We were asked whether or not we wanted to go to Canungra and because I had been in the tropics for the last twelve months they were prepared to give us an exemption, which both Paul Mench and myself took, and I ended up arriving in country about 17 January 1967.[26]

Ben described the training and preparation at the Reinforcement Wing in Ingleburn, Sydney, as 'ad hoc', adding, 'There didn't seem to be a real plan; there just seemed to be a lot of turmoil. So the training was fairly disjointed.'[27] However, he thought that he was reasonably well prepared for active service:

> I was, due to the fact that I had just spent twelve months in Papua New Guinea, and I think there were also parts of the RMC syllabus that stood us in good stead. In Second

Class we did a first aid course and I used that to save men
in Viet Nam.[28]

Ben's first appointment after arriving in the 1st Australian
Reinforcement Unit in Nui Dat was in the Civil Affairs
Unit, which he discovered hadn't had an administration
officer since its inception. His duties revolved around
providing assistance and liaison to the local ARVN posts
where the Australian Task Force had regional advisers, and
as Ben explained, 'we helped them with their civil affairs'.
Ben detailed some of the jobs he had:

> If a cordon and search was on, Civil Affairs turned up
> with the Psyops equipment and ready to set up to supple-
> ment the doctors or had their own doctors; it was very
> much an ad hoc thing and if problems were identified
> during the Medcaps and Dentcaps [dental civil aid pro-
> jects], part of our job was to follow up and get the people
> into Ba Ria for medical and dental treatment.[29]

His job took him all over the old Phuoc Tuy Province, and
most of the time he travelled alone with just a sidearm
and a 7.62 mm SLR (self-loading rifle) for company. By
February 1967, Ben was posted to 5 RAR as a reinforcement officer. He recalled what it was like joining the
battalion as a reo:

> Well the first thing is that you are going in alone and you
> feel that ... They had been together in country for about
> seven or eight months. You are the new boy on the block.
> The other thing is because you are in Viet Nam on
> company-sized operations you don't get to know the rest

of the battalion officers. I met some of them Thursday
week ago [February 2005] in Canberra! We were in the
same battalion but we didn't get to meet because they
happened to be in C Company or D Company.[30]

After another stint with the Civil Affairs unit, Ben found
himself posted to 2 RAR, again as a reinforcement officer.
This time the experience was far from pleasant:

> The OC there treated me like one of those people who
> hadn't won the war. 'We are here to win the war, you are
> one of those losers who hadn't won it up till now' type of
> thing, and that is a pretty hard attitude to overcome. And
> in some ways if I had been someone with not as much
> experience as I had, I would have just buckled under just
> from that attitude.[31]

Ben described his time with 2 RAR as 'tough'. He was
involved in a bad mine incident when working with the
unit in late November 1967, and the man who triggered
the 'Jumping Jack' (M-16) mine was killed instantly. It is
probably fair to say that Ben would not have undertaken a
pilgrimage with people from 2 RAR because of the underlying emotions of his experience with that unit.

Ben enjoyed his time with 5 RAR, which he described
as 'happy. I enjoyed that platoon and I think they enjoyed
me.' He believed the battalion was 'very professional;
they knew what they were on about; they didn't take silly
risks'. Ben added, 'They were there to stay alive but they
were also there to win a war. They had a respect for men's
lives.'[32]

When the Australians withdrew from South Viet Nam in 1972, Ben felt that 'we [as an Army] had been let down. We had been let down by the politicians who had tied our hands behind our fucking backs and not let us get on with the war.' The pain of that conflict was still highly evident as he continued, 'I am still sure in my own mind that if we had been left to run the war the way it should have been, we would have won it.' When the South inevitably fell in 1975 he felt 'sad, because a lot of good people were going to get hurt'.[33]

It is a fair assumption that Ben has post traumatic stress disorder (PTSD), but he works hard at managing it. He has not let it stop him from returning to Viet Nam—when he joined the 5 RAR tour group it was his fourth visit back since the war. 'I want to come to peace with the country and I can't do that by just doing one visit,' he explained.[34] Ben's other trips were privately organised tours in December 1997 and January 1998 with his partner, who is now his second wife. His reactions from the first trip were not easy to deal with, and he believed he needed to return a third time in July 1999 to where he served, 'just to stand and reflect'.[35]

Ben's wife Jenny accompanied him on the trip in October 2005. He wanted to show her 'the Army side of Viet Nam' by being on a trip with Army colleagues, as Jenny has never been 'an Army wife', as Ben put it, and 'didn't understand a lot of Army things'.[36]

Ben's expectations on the October 2005 5 RAR tour were 'not all that great . . . just to go back and come to some sort of peace with the whole place'.[37] I asked Ben if he had any apprehensions, and he said he thought that the group would experience 'reactions', based upon his own experiences on previous tours. As it happened, I don't think this was the case, and veterans should be aware that everyone reacts differently to what they see, smell, hear and feel when they are back in Viet Nam. One cannot throw a blanket over a group and say that they will feel a certain way: we are too complex and have had too many life experiences to simplify an emotive reaction.

Today, Ben lives in Wollongong and is still serving with the Army Reserve in the RAAMC.

Captain Fred Pfitzner, Company Second-in-Command, 5 RAR; Operations Officer, 1 ATF Headquarters

Square-framed and muscular, Fred Pfitzner is a big bloke who stands a tad over 183 cm (6 feet). He was born in Adelaide into a large family of nine kids and moved to Canberra in 1959 to attend RMC Duntroon, where he graduated in 1962. He saw active service in Malaya and Borneo as a rifle platoon commander with 3 RAR, returning to Australia skilled in jungle warfare in 1965. While serving with the 28th Commonwealth Brigade in Singapore, along with many officers Fred did a two-week reconnaissance to South Viet Nam and was made familiar with the operational scenario in country. After posting to the 6 Task Force at Enoggera Barracks in Brisbane, he was initially told he was going as a reinforcement officer to serve as a captain in operations in the Task Force headquarters, but that was changed to a company second-in-command in 5 RAR once the 'powers that be' realised that the blokes working in the command post should have some idea of what was going on out 'in the weeds'.

Arriving in the unit was not as daunting for him as it was for most other officer reinforcements because, as Fred recalled, he knew the man who met him at Nui Dat: '[Major] Blue Hodgkinson and I had spent nine of my first thirteen years in the Army together; he was my company commander in Malaya.' His flight over was interesting: 'I was the DCO [draft conducting officer] on a Qantas flight via Manila with a whole bunch of people I didn't know, and only another one or two officers. Maintaining decorum in Manila was not easy.' The 24-year-old Captain Pfitzner admitted to being 'excited' about entering another war zone—it was a feeling of 'once more into the breach; that was what I was being paid for'.[38]

Fred's company commander was Major Bruce McQualter, who tragically died of wounds sustained in a mine incident in the Long Hai Hills on 22 February 1967, about seven months into the tour. Fred added, 'We lost two officers in that one and about nine Diggers and 22 wounded, from memory.' The loss of two officers from 5 RAR plus the forward observer gutted the rifle company: 'Well, they were rooted; they were pulled back straight after it ... They were literally a rump of a company and they were employed on minefield security while it was being built until they went home.'[39]

Fred then saw out the remainder of his tour from May to December 1967 as an operations officer in the Task

Force headquarters working on shift in the command post, and as the Task Force patrol master coordinating TAOR (tactical area of responsibility) patrols. Fred recalls wryly:

> It wasn't hard; it was 24 hours a day, seven days a week. There were periods of intense activity and every now and then you could relax a bit, like in any bloody war. There were a few peaks like the first time we started operating east of Dat Do and things like that, which represented a significant change in the capability of the Task Force, being able to operate away from its own close protection.[40]

The pilgrimage with 5 RAR was to be Fred's first return to Viet Nam. He assumed 'that the countryside will be as lovely as it ever was, the girls will look much the same'. Fred knew that 70 per cent of the population was born after the war, 'so they aren't going to be too interested in a fat-arsed bunch of old farts running around'. He was also hoping to see, even though the Socialist Republic of Viet Nam is a Communist country, 'that entrepreneurial streak—especially in the South—that was always there'. He added with a smile, 'They are like the Chinese; they are all basically capitalists.'[41]

Fred had few qualms about returning, but also knew much had changed in areas where he had served (his greatest apprehension was leaving his farm outside Canberra, with his Murray Grey breeders about to start calving). Fred was one of many who were disappointed about the withdrawal of Australians from the war in 1972, especially as he was then commanding a ready reaction force—called Fred Force (Alpha Company 9 RAR)—to deploy to South Viet Nam if things 'got untidy' with the remnants of the Australian force left in Saigon. On the fall of Saigon and the collapse of resistance to the National Liberation Front offensive in 1975, Fred stated he was 'disappointed in the sense that we lost, and resigned in the sense that it was probably ever going to be so'.

Like many warriors who served in Phuoc Tuy Province and other areas in South Viet Nam, Fred is proud of his service. He didn't think the war was a lost cause:

> Not when we were there, no. In fact I think that the Australian Army can still to this day hold its head up about its conduct of operations in Phuoc Tuy, especially in the early days because they got on top of the problem and provided the firm base from which operations were able to be launched out of the province, and we didn't ever have our hands on the back door, which could have happened.[42]

Today retired brigadier Fred Pfitzner—who describes himself as a 'prickle farmer'—and his wife Helen grow Murray Grey breeders on an acreage outside Canberra and keep a weather eye out for rain that may one day again fall on this parched nation.

Captain Ron Shambrook, Quartermaster, Company Commander and Company Second-in-Command, 5 RAR

When Cairns-born Ron Shambrook turned eighteen, he went straight into the CMF and shortly after that National Service (the first scheme in the 1950s). He was promoted to second lieutenant in 1953 and later became a company commander. Cairns then, like all other CMF units, changed when the Army adopted what was known as the Pentropic organisation.[43] Cairns lost its battalion and Townsville was the centre for the 2nd Battalion, Royal Queensland Regiment (2 RQR), which was one of three battalions that previously formed the 11th Brigade. When this reorganisation came to the Militia Army in 1963, Ron was basically out of a job in uniform. As he put it, 'I had the opportunity to join the Regular Army, and I did.'[44] He was recommended for Regular Service and took the plunge after talking with his wife Elizabeth. Ron was posted to 1 RAR at Holsworthy and, as was the custom in those days, this substantive major had to drop a rank and was now a captain in the Australian Regular Army.

At this time 1 RAR were aware unofficially that they might be deploying to Viet Nam and Ron wanted to stay with 1 RAR. The 5th Battalion was about to be raised and Lieutenant Colonel John Warr, who was the battalion Executive Officer of 1 RAR and was about to be made CO of 5 RAR, said to Ron, 'I want you to be my Quartermaster in 5 RAR.'[45] Despite 33-year-old Ron's protestations and lack of quartermaster training, he was given the task of raising the indents to crank up 5 RAR from a stores perspective. It was a monumental task, and one that Ron found one of the most frustrating but also rewarding jobs in his career.

Ron had been to New Guinea but had never been to Asia. He said, 'There was excitement, I wanted to be there.' Ron's tour diary in Viet Nam reads like a 'Rent a Captain' bouncing from one job to another. The CO kept his promise after the battalion was settled in and Ron went off to a rifle company as a company second-in-command, then acting company commander of Administration Company, followed by a stint in Task Force headquarters. After he was promoted to major he ended up commanding Charlie Company 5 RAR.

Like Fred Pfitzner, this was to be Ron's first trip back. Unfortunately his wife Elizabeth fell ill just before departure and had to stay home, which was a great disappointment to both Ron and his wife. When asked why he wanted his wife to accompany him, Ron explained the catalysts for his decision to return:

> I wanted to take Elizabeth back and show her some of the areas. Up until last year I had no intention of going back at all. We were sitting in Wagga at the RSL after having laid up the colours of 5 RAR the night before. Half a dozen of us suddenly brought up this suggestion of going back as a pilgrimage rather than as a tourist and it snowballed from there. And now I am excited to be going back. I don't particularly want to go and see the American War in Viet Nam, I would rather go and see what we did, and remember those colleagues; we had 25 dead and about 100 casualties.[46]

Ron expected the country to have changed significantly, but was still looking forward to visiting places like Nui Dat. Asked if he had any apprehensions, he said:

> I am certain it will pull a few emotional chords at certain places. I have done a lot of touring in recent years and

there will be some of that. I am looking forward to North Viet Nam and the northern part of [South] Viet Nam, which we didn't see because we didn't win. [Chuckles.][47]

Ron was sad at the outcome of the war, and not just from a military perspective; the loss of lives on both sides was dreadful and a cause for regret.

Today Ron and Elizabeth live in retirement in Brisbane.

Captain John Taske, RMO

John Taske served in South Viet Nam as an RMO with several units including 5 RAR, 6 RAR, 1 Field Regiment, Royal Australian Artillery (RAA) and 8 Field Ambulance. John is an adventurous man who made the military his career after medical training, retiring with the rank of colonel. He was accompanied for most of the trip to Viet Nam in 2005 by his second wife Tina, who had to leave the tour before it finished to attend a conference elsewhere overseas.

This was John's first trip back to Viet Nam. His main reasons for joining the pilgrimage were:

To have a holiday, renew old friendships, see those parts of Vietnam that I saw on my tour of duty, and see what changes time and peace have brought. I also want to see parts of the country that I haven't seen before.[48]

While John had no apprehensions about his return visit, he had another major reason for having his wife Tina on the trip: 'Because Tina wasn't with me when I was in the Army, she has no idea of the Army, or the blokes, or what I did.'[49]

As an RMO, John had seen the harsher side of the conflict—what is often described as the debris of war. He said that when his time was up, he was 'glad to be going home after having done my bit'. When the Australians withdrew in 1972, he felt:

> ... deep anger with the politicians who had ordered Australian troops up there to help the South Vietnamese repel Communism and give them a chance to attain democracy; but then when those troops had, at great mental and physical cost, achieved everything that had been asked of them, pulled the rug out from under their feet and made all their efforts—the lives and limbs lost; the fears, nightmares, psychological damage to so many— worthless.[50]

John doesn't mince words and he wrote that his chief concern when the South fell in 1975 was that the South Vietnamese people had 'been used—betrayed in the worst possible way, by the politicians of the US and Australia, the media of both countries, the Jane Fondas and other ignorant, bleeding-heart do-gooders'.[51] Tina said she came on the trip 'to support my husband, who has been talking about Viet Nam since I met him, and I had no understanding—absolutely no understanding—of what Viet Nam was and what it meant to him'.[52]

Today John resides and works as a consultant anaesthetist in Brisbane.

Lieutenant Roger Wainwright, Platoon Commander, Bravo Company, 5 RAR

Roger Wainwright was another RMC Duntroon graduate in 1965 who eventually made the Army his career. He had served in school cadets and when he saw Steve Gower—now the Director of the Australian War Memorial and a retired major general, who was a close family friend and was at school with his brother—coming back from RMC on leave where he was the senior under officer and had won the Sword of Honour and the Queens Medal, he thought, 'Well if he can do it, so can I.' Roger adds with a laugh, 'But it didn't happen that way.'[53] Roger is an infantryman through and through, and he and John Hartley (also later to retire as a major general) were the first graduates from RMC to be posted to the newly formed 5 RAR. He described his knowledge of the war in South Viet Nam while a cadet as 'very sparse', adding, 'And even though 1 RAR had deployed there in April/May 1965 there was very little interest [by the cadets].'[54] However, his knowledge of it rapidly grew as his unit prepared for the war:

> The training that we did was very much getting into counter-revolutionary warfare and obviously taking lessons from the Malaya campaign and Confrontation and those sorts of things. We were out in the close training around Holsworthy pretty soon; I can remember doing platoon attacks; they had us in fairly thick areas around the Holsworthy Range. We did the training up at Canungra and I think we were the first battalion to go up there and

do that. The good thing I remember about it was the CO had put a lot of emphasis on section and platoon-level stuff so we got to know our own people pretty well, and the last two or three days on the exercise at Gospers Plateau was as a company and in the company environment.[55]

Roger recalls their deployment to South Viet Nam as one of 'firsts'. His platoon was the first one to fly out of Richmond, and the first infantry platoon of the Task Force (not counting 1 RAR, who were never in 1 ATF) on the ground in Viet Nam. He recalled the 'tension, excitement and expectation' among his soldiers on the plane flying into Saigon, stating, 'I think everyone realised that we were going into the unknown.'[56] Roger's platoon saw a fair amount of action in South Viet Nam, and most of his men survived the fifteen or so contacts they had with the enemy. He was saddened by the loss of one man killed and fourteen wounded in action, of whom four had to be returned to Australia.

I asked Roger if it was a good experience for him, going to the war, and he replied: 'Yes. As a professional soldier, you did what you had to; you proved things to yourself.' He added, 'I mean how you handled yourself under pressure; how you lead people; if you kill people on the other side, how you react. And how you react when your own people are killed or badly wounded, and your relationships.'[57]

As President of the 5 RAR Battalion Association, Roger was the driving force behind the 2005 pilgrimage. It was his first trip back and one thing he really wanted to do was return to where his company headquarters was decimated by a landmine incident that killed his company commander, the company second-in-command, the forward observer, and wounded many more in company headquarters outside a small village called An Nhut. In a paradoxical way he also wanted to find out if going back was what he really wanted to do. As he explained, 'If it turns out that I end up saying, "Gee, I wish I hadn't done this trip", then at least I will know.'[58]

Roger's wife of 36 years, Tina, accompanied Roger on the pilgrimage. When asked why, she replied:

> I think curiosity more than anything else. I've also had a connection with my sister having lived in Saigon during the war, so I was interested to have a look at Saigon now. But mostly having heard all of Roger's stories—names of places, names of battles, names of things that happened to him—I was interested to be here and that's something I can share with him.[59]

Tina Wainwright was also not sure how Roger's emotions would hold up when he went back to places like An Nhut that she knew would be emotionally challenging. Looking at Roger during their post-tour interview she stated simply, 'I wanted to be here to support him . . . if he needed it.'[60]

Today Roger lives in Canberra and works as a consultant to the Department of Defence.

Captain Tony White, RMO, 5 RAR

Tony White was the third doctor in the 5 RAR pilgrimage tour. He was accompanied by his wife, Doffy, and 32-year-old son, Rupert. Tony's family has a history of military service and two of his male relatives (John and Peter White) gained honour and recognition serving with the AATTV and the RAR respectively. Tony and Doffy had been to Viet Nam in 2002 attending a medical conference in Hanoi, and then did the 'obligatory tourist circuit—Ha Long Bay, Da Nang, Hué, Hoi An and home via Saigon'. This would be his first return to the area where he served as the RMO in 5 RAR. When asked why he had decided to come on the trip he replied:

> This—39 years on—is a long overdue pilgrimage to the scene of the single most important and vivid year of my life. The size and make-up of the party is ideal—brother officers and spouses plus a historical backbone [the author] to keep us honest. I expect that we'll have plenty of time, over the odd Bier 333, to rake over what the hell it was all about. I'm particularly proud that my son, Rupert, is accompanying us to deepen his knowledge of this slice of our family's history.[61]

Tony was pragmatic about what the countryside would be like when he returned to what was once called Phuoc Tuy Province, remarking, 'I don't expect much to be recognisable at either Nui Dat or Vung Tau, but know that certain things—the heat and humidity, the smell of tropical decay, rice paddies, the silhouette of the Warburtons—will be quite unchanged.'[62] Asked whether he had any apprehensions, Tony replied: 'No, I have no worries. I feel that I've fully digested the events of my year of active service, and would be surprised by the emergence of any ghosts—but who knows until you get there?'[63]

Tony was looking forward to 'the companionship of this small, wonderful group. I relish learning other people's perspectives on common experiences and expect to hear some great stories.' He added:

> This was a very convenient moment because here was a group of fellow officers in the same unit, which I think is much more important than having just a bunch of mixed veterans. And Doffy agreed to come and I was very, very happy that Rupert also agreed to come. So it was a wonderful opportunity and not one to pass over.[64]

He was also keen to see what the locals are now making of their lives in the villages, and added sombrely, 'I look forward to a minute's silence among the columns and rows of a rubber plantation.'[65]

Like many who spent a year on active service and witnessed the brutality and horrors of war, Captain White was elated on his last day on active service as he choppered out of Luscombe Field airstrip onto the deck of HMAS *Sydney*. He recalled that he was 'mentally exhausted by the end of the tour and, like everyone else, at the end of my tether'. When the South fell in 1975, Tony was:

> Deeply saddened by the finality and the futility of all those lost or damaged lives; all the solid duty put in by so many in the belief that they were on the 'right' side and all now brought to zilch by this crushing defeat.[66]

Tony had heard a lot from other veterans who'd done trips back to Viet Nam. In hindsight he reflected, 'I was expecting a rather limited and more threadbare experience than what it has been.'[67]

Doffy White 'came with a very open mind', but admitted, 'I was very nervous about being with the group and I thought really that I could be an extraneous person and I felt nervous about coming as a spouse.'[68] She added that Tony had been asked to write a paper about a mine incident, and this was something of a catalyst for the family coming to Viet Nam together:

> I just felt that I had heard so many stories from so many other people, not a lot from Tony until the last few years, until he'd written the story about the mine. And after that came out he started making contact with people that I hadn't met or just met very briefly. And I just sort of felt that there was a surge of knowledge that I needed to sort of come and clarify as well. Just to see where all these things were, to put them in context, to smell it, to feel it, to understand.[69]

Only occasionally do children accompany their veteran parents on tours to Viet Nam. Son Rupert was very keen, explaining:

> Well, I had a thought; I always used to play with my old man's Army gear. He just had a duffle bag and loads of 8-mm film. I've always seen that quite a bit and Dad's been pretty good, detailing various things about his operational time. And when I got an invitation to this, I jumped at it.[70]

However, Rupert was also a little anxious about slotting into the group. 'I was actually a bit nervous about coming along. I thought I might disturb the group a little bit, as far as all the guys getting together. If they wanted to let stuff out maybe they wouldn't.'[71] As it turned out, Rupert's fears were unfounded and he was made most welcome by the group.

Today Dr Tony White lives in Randwick, Sydney, and is a practising dermatologist.

—m—

Once the group had decided to do the pilgrimage, they then set about determining the style of tour they would have, their basic and then later detailed itinerary, and how they would incorporate all the participants' individual requirements, as they all had various things they wanted to see and do. Roger Wainwright was primarily responsible for coordinating that aspect and making sure as many people as possible were satisfied.

The majority of the group would assemble in Sydney after flying or driving in from Canberra, New South Wales and Queensland. Others would join the group in Singapore and in Saigon. They would stay several days in Ho Chi Minh City, then take the hydrofoil down the Saigon River to Vung Tau and base themselves out of the resort town for several days while they visited the old Phuoc Tuy Province sites like Nui Dat, Long Tan, Binh Ba and the Long Hai Hills. They would then return by road to Saigon, fly to Da Nang and take some R&C in the beautiful seaside town of Hoi An after visiting Marble Mountain and Red Beach. Refreshed and relaxed they would then emplane a couple of days later for the national capital. In

Hanoi they would finish their tour with an overnight trip out to Ha Long Bay and then return home.

Once the itinerary was sorted out Garry Adams and I briefed the group on what they could expect so that nobody had any false expectations. In October 2005, most of the group assembled in Sydney to fly out, and then met up with others (like Peter Isaacs, travelling from Europe) in Viet Nam.

They were off and running.

Part II

A PILGRIMAGE

Chapter 3

HO CHI MINH CITY (SAIGON) AND SURROUNDS

Most visitors to Viet Nam, whether they are on a pilgrimage or simply a holiday, will want to see its largest city, which locals still call Saigon—although they tend to use the word to describe the inner city or central business district, and not the newer outerlying districts that have sprung up since 1976, when it was renamed Ho Chi Minh City. Those returning to this bustling metropolis will notice the changes at the airport and the expansion of the sprawling suburbs around the former Southern capital. What hasn't changed is the heat, humidity and the overpowering smell of the tropics. Even in the cooler wet season this is still a hot place to visit.

Most servicemen and women did not see too much of Saigon during the war unless they were serving in the Headquarters of the Australian Forces Vietnam or a related subsidiary headquarters. When soldiers were departing on rest and recuperation (R&R) leave they usually left South Viet Nam via Saigon and often overnighted at the temporary accommodation US Forces' billet known as Camp Alpha. Saigon was the military hub of operations and the seat of government in South Viet Nam, and saw vicious fighting during the Tet Offensive in early 1968. Its capture by Communist forces in 1975 marked the end of the Viet Nam War.

Today Ho Chi Minh City is a sprawling, industrious, madcap metropolis of over 6 million people—and many of them are on 120cc motorcycles. Noisy, energetic and colourful, it is the commercial capital of Viet Nam and a bit more expensive than the rest of the country.

There are still many sights and places of interest to see in the city and the reader is directed to books such as the Lonely Planet guide and *Australia's Battlefields in Viet Nam*[1] for greater detail than can be included here. Saigon is a great place to kick off a pilgrimage because a few days in this vibrant city allows you to acclimatise, adjust to being in an Asian environment where road rules are totally ignored, and for those who want to shop it allows a quick comparison to be done early so best buys are guaranteed later in the tour. It also allows the traveller to conduct day trips to places like the Cu Chi tunnels, an overnight trip to the Delta and to visit the various museums in the city itself.

Visiting Cu Chi just north-west of the city can be unsettling as the veteran will find himself back in the bush again walking down jungle paths to visit various aspects of this now popular tourist attraction. The Vietnamese are particularly proud of their achievements during the American War, especially the fact that a Viet Cong division was able to operate and survive so close to Saigon for the duration of the war. However, there are times when the veteran will feel insulted by the way the war is portrayed here, especially in the propaganda film that is shown in a theatrette at the tunnel site. And veterans should also be aware that even though the tunnels have been widened to accommodate larger Westerners, they can be claustrophobic for some, and a bitter reminder to others who had to enter and clear tunnels during the war. Just outside the Cu Chi tourist complex is a large shrine that honours some 50 000 Viet Cong soldiers from the region who lost their lives; it is well worth a visit.

The veteran is also warned that the War Remnants Museum in Ho Chi Minh City is particularly confronting and clearly biased in its approach to war atrocities, where only the 'American imperialists' and the accompanying 'puppets' are portrayed as committing misdeeds. There is no coverage of Viet Cong terrorism, or the savage National Liberation Front butchery in cities like Hué during the 1968 Tet Offensive. But that is something to be accepted as part of Viet Nam's reunification and not intended as a slight against the individual veteran.

As Peter Isaacs wrote after his visit in 2005 about the official government slant on history and events:

I didn't read anything in the War Remnants Museum in Saigon that was an obvious lie—but the story portrayed is totally one-sided. At the 'Hanoi Hilton' prison in Hanoi, there is a marble tablet which proclaims how US POWs received 'adequate food and clothing' and were treated humanely. They won the war, why do they feel it necessary to lie? The short history of Vietnam printed in the tourist guide in the seat pocket of the Vietnam Airlines aircraft that conveyed us from Da Nang to Hanoi states that the country has had three distinct periods of history. The most recent was the declaration of Independence from colonial rule by President Ho Chi Minh in 1945. No mention at all of subsequent events.[2]

But a visit to Ho Chi Minh City is not all doom and gloom. It is a city that unrelentingly pulsates with life—24 hours a day. There is non-stop traffic, non-stop activity and it boasts good restaurants, interesting attractions and represents Asia at its most colourful.

Peter Rogers has been back to Viet Nam several times and his first return to Ho Chi Minh City simply stunned him: 'we couldn't get over the number of motorcycles and when you want to cross the road, you need steely resolve: just step off the kerb and just go for it and don't stop.'[3] What Peter is referring to is the 'river of humanity' flowing around you as literally hundreds of cyclists and commuters on motorcycles zoom past in what seems to be a never-ending flow. There are few pedestrian crossings—and they would be ignored anyway unless a traffic policeman was operating on that intersection. Once you step off the pavement you are like a rock in a creek, and if you stop you are as good as dead. So the advice is to watch out, but just keep walking across the road at a steady pace. And please, don't stop!

Tan Son Nhut international airport

The absolute thing one could not avoid when landing in Viet Nam during the war was the tropical climate. That heavy, heady mixture of high heat, oppressive humidity, and the odours of an Asian city was like having a warm, wet, smelly blanket thrown over your body. You breathed in the moist air and your nostrils flared, your head snapped back as the reek of rotting vegetation, open drains and sewers combined to make your eyes water, and you wished you hadn't had lunch.

For many Australian servicemen, Saigon's Tan Son Nhut airport was their first point of entry to the Viet Nam War and will undoubtedly bring back memories for veterans returning today.

Tan Son Nhut was huge in area and very high in aircraft movement during the war. It combined civilian and military air traffic, although the vast majority was military during the time of Australia's involvement in the conflict. Literally hundreds of military aircraft were permanently located on the airbase, and a three-metre-high wall topped with barbed wire encircled the entire airfield. Aircraft were stored in sandbagged concrete revetments, and some were housed in open-ended concrete hangars. The remains of those reinforced hangars are still evident today. Trying to photograph these war relics will result in your camera (and film if relevant) being confiscated, as Tan Son Nhut is still an operational airbase for the Socialist Republic of Viet Nam air force.

Australia's national airline Qantas was chartered to deploy many of the individual reinforcements and replacement personnel to South Viet Nam, with almost half of the Australians carried by Qantas charter jet. The Boeing 707 aircraft usually flew out of Sydney, and were scheduled to arrive at Tan Son Nhut airport around mid-morning and to depart with returning personnel several hours later. Initially the aircraft staged through Manila, but later flew via Singapore after diplomatic arrangements for the transit of Australian service personnel were made with a somewhat reticent Singaporean government.

There is an old joke that goes, 'How did you find [insert a country or place]?' And the jokester will answer, 'I got off the plane and there it was.' And anyone who flew into Tan Son Nhut on the Qantas charter can tell you what they remember about the first time they stuck their head out of the 707. Derrill De Heer recalled:

> I had been in Asia before and I expected the smells to be there again. They weren't as bad as Singapore and Malacca in 1962. My most vivid memory was the number of planes at the airport. Fighters like F-4 Phantoms, helicopters— load carrying and gunships. Transport aircraft—C-123, C-130, C-117, OV-10 Broncos, etc. I couldn't get over how close they were to each other. Many in the open, many in arming bays and others under overhead protection with side revetments. I was surprised at the number of civilians working in and around the airport. All wearing black pyjamas. When I was at the Infantry Centre we were told the enemy wore black pyjamas. We were surrounded! I got over that easily, but a number who hadn't been overseas before were seen to be nervous.[4]

Captain and Quartermaster Ron Shambrook first flew into Tan Son Nhut as part of the 5 RAR advance party in 1966. He had been to Asia before, but when he looked out across the tarmac he couldn't believe his eyes:

I guess the biggest impression when I landed at Tan Son Nhut was the American air equipment that was there. Be they helicopters, be they all sorts of shapes and sizes of aircraft, many of which I had never seen before. The revetments that were around some of them; the activity by the Americans, and that was clearly the most significant thing.[5]

Pilot Peter Rogers was on his way to join the 161 Recce Flight in Nui Dat and was craning his neck to look out the 707 jet window. Peter remembered what he was taking in through excited eyes:

My most vivid memory is of flying really low and steep into Tan Son Nhut. I could see the craters from aerial bombs, artillery and whatever . . . and looking out and thinking, 'Oh God, it looks like we are in a war zone.'[6]

Captain Ted Heffernan was posted as a medical officer to the artillery field regiment and also to serve in the field ambulance at Nui Dat. He was given the desultory pre-deployment briefings at Healesville and Canungra and recalled looking out into the glare of the tropical haze as he stepped onto the aircraft stairs in 1966:

We had a briefing at Puckapunyal and my understanding of it was that you would know who were Viet Cong because they wore black pyjamas—when we landed at Saigon everyone had black pyjamas on, and we thought we were too late![7]

Some soldiers flying into Saigon found themselves in a war zone much sooner than they expected. Infantryman

Second Lieutenant Neil Weekes flew into South Viet Nam as part of the 1 RAR advance party in early 1968. Neil wrote in a letter:

> When we arrived at the airport, Saigon was under attack. There was artillery fire going in, fires around the airport. There were several damaged planes that had been hit with rocket or artillery fire, and as we got off the plane we were issued our weapons and live rounds for our magazines. We were then shown across to the protection bays of the aircraft where we huddled against the walls while waiting for a couple of Caribou to fly us into Nui Dat—my diary records, 'Guns blasting everywhere—we're in it.'[8]

Most units, other than the infantry battalions, used what was called a 'trickle reinforcement system' to replace their soldiers when their tour of duty was completed. Cavalryman Ross McCormack recalled his arrival at Tan Son Nhut in 1970:

> As the aircraft descended to land at Saigon, I remember the green paddy fields of the Delta area soon changed to the harsh realities of Tan Son Nhut airport, with all sorts of military aircraft coming and going. The noise was continuous, the smell of aircraft exhaust was overpowering, and the temperature and humidity debilitating. I was at Tan Son Nhut for about three hours before I was able to jump on board a Caribou 'Wallaby' flight to Nui Dat.[9]

Tan Son Nhut today is like many other international airports with its multi-storey construction, chrome and glass fittings, baggage carousels and airbridges. The only frustrating thing about moving through the airport complex is what seems like the inordinate amount of time to be processed through Customs and Immigration, however that unfortunately seems to be the case anywhere around the globe in the new millennium.

Coral and Balmoral battle sites

In May 1968 the Australian Task Force was redeployed out of Phuoc Tuy Province and tasked to sit astride a main ingress route into Saigon about 35 kilometres from the capital and twenty kilometres north of Bien Hoa City. The 1st and 3rd Battalions RAR found themselves facing a numerically superior force on the north-western approach route for almost a month as they occupied and fought out of Fire Support Bases Coral and Balmoral respectively during what became known as the second Tet Offensive. The two fire support bases were only six kilometres apart and able to support each other with troops, tanks and field artillery.

Veterans of the Fire Support Base Coral and Balmoral battles are advised that the areas where they fought so tenaciously against the Viet Cong in May 1968 are now working rubber plantations, and are regarded by the Vietnamese government as 'sensitive sites'. There are now large obelisk monuments at the sites honouring the Viet Cong soldiers who died in the battles. At the Coral site is a crypt that holds the remains of about 41 Viet Cong soldiers who were buried in a mass grave by the Australians.[10]

To visit the battle sites requires a permit that travel companies need to organise in advance with the government's tourist organisation and which must be carried by visitors. It is also customary to visit the local People's District Committee beforehand as a courtesy before entering the sites.

I was on such a visit in 2002 and mistakenly believed that the tourist company had issued my guide with permits for both sites, but found myself detained at the local police station for an afternoon as only one battle site was covered by the permit. Spending an afternoon at gunpoint in a holding room is not everyone's idea of a good time, so it pays to make sure with your guide and travel company that your permits cover all 'sensitive sites' you intend to visit. When in doubt, ask at the local police station. You may find a 'fee' will allow you unfettered access. Enough said.

The Mekong Delta

During the war, the Mekong Delta to the south of Ho Chi Minh City was the preserve of the brown water navies of the Republic of (South) Viet Nam and the US Navy SEAL (Sea Air and Land) commando teams, the US Marine Corps and US Special Forces soldiers. The Allies relied principally on amphibious and heliborne operations, with Australian support in the form of the AATTV, Canberra bomber crews on air strike missions, forward air controllers, and Royal Australian diving teams who helped clear stakes, booby traps and mines from the many waterways that created dangerous obstacles for Allied patrol craft. The enemy were also heavily engaged in the destruction of bridges, using floating birdcage mines with timed fuses.

Travelling south to the Mekong Delta region has been fraught with problems in recent years mainly owing to poor roads, unreliable ferry services and communication difficulties. However, within a year or so it is anticipated that trips down to the Delta will become more frequent. There is a lot of flat, green empty space to look at on that voyage, apart from the ribbon development on each side of the road. Unless there is a special reason for seeing the area, a single overnight trip will usually suffice to satisfy the curious.

Peter Rogers and his wife Suzie visited the Delta region, and although Peter never served there he did find it interesting:

> Down on the Delta, where people live their whole lives on their boats, was something else. It is a land of contrasts and is totally different to what most Diggers remember, and that is reason enough for going back to my mind.[11]

Chapter 4

INSIDE THE WIRE: NUI DAT

The Nui Dat base

The Australian Task Force base at Nui Dat was 'home' for a year for the vast majority of soldiers who served in South Viet Nam. The base was sited centrally in Phuoc Tuy Province around Nui Dat hill (Nui Dat is Vietnamese for 'small hill'). It was astride the main arterial road, Provincial Route 2, an all-weather road that ran from the provincial capital of Ba Ria (also called Phuoc Le) to the Long Khanh Province border. Being only 30 kilometres from the logistic support base at the port of Vung Tau, it was an ideal location and all that was needed to occupy the site was to clear the locals out of the immediate vicinity and construct a bypass road. Positioning the main base in the centre of the province, away from the main population concentration in Ba Ria, suited the operational counter-revolutionary warfare plans and greatly hindered the Viet Cong's intelligence-gathering opportunities. The area was relatively flat and was mostly covered in rubber plantations. The well-groomed avenues of trees had provided steady work for several villages in the local area.

The soldiers arrived in Nui Dat by several means. Some flew in by Caribou after transferring from chartered

Qantas 707 jet airliners at Tan Son Nhut airport, landing at what was named Luscombe Field. Some came in by road in the backs of trucks. Others flew off the HMAS *Sydney* in US Army Chinook CH-47 helicopters, like Bill Kromwyk. He recalled arriving at Nui Dat airstrip in 1969:

> The adrenaline was running high: here we are, we are actually in Viet Nam. And you were expecting trouble straightaway, like are we going to get shot at? Are there any mortars coming in? We just didn't know what to expect, so we were wary at all times, but of course nothing happened and it was actually a very peaceful entry into Viet Nam. And then we made our way to our lines and where we were going to be camped and were allocated our four-man tents. From Luscombe airfield we just walked down to our lines.[1]

Regardless of how you arrived, you had heard about 'The Dat'. It was going to be your home for the next 365 days . . . and a wakey. Derrill De Heer looked around him and remembered later that 'the dust at Nui Dat was a bit surprising'. Coming in on the advance party for 8 RAR, he was to be billeted by the outgoing 9th Battalion. He recalled, 'I was there when the soldier fragged the officer [Lieutenant Convery] with a grenade. It was a scary few days as the person had vowed to kill a few other people in his company.'[2]

But not all new arrivals had such an unsettling reception. Staff Sergeant Bob Hann's main memory of landing at Nui Dat after being ferried via Chinook choppers from Vung Tau was 'the heat and the smell'.[3] Ian Ryan came in by military convoy in the back of a truck. This was his first time in a war zone and his first quick impressions of the area were: '[It was] hot; the different landscape, the people, the military activity and the uncanny realisation of the unknown, and how important our training was going to be.'[4]

When 5 RAR first swept through the area on Operation Hardihood in late May 1966, Nui Dat was a recently abandoned rubber plantation, with clear ground between the rows of trees and good visibility. There was no airstrip that later dominated the geographical landscape of the base. There were no huts, kitchens or aluminium huts. It was just a rubber plantation.

Roger Wainwright recalled going into the area on his first deployment, his memory of it still crystal clear, aided by the map he has kept from that operation. Their first contact with the enemy was:

> On Day 1, up near An Phu, right up near where 5 RAR eventually had its headquarters. There was a little cemetery up there where the mortar platoon was deployed and that was where we had the first contact. We flew into LZ [Landing Zone] Hudson, which was on the western side of An Phu village.[5]

The battalion had to start from scratch in establishing what would be their home for the next eleven months. Not only did the surrounding area need to be secured, but the base as well. This was no easy task owing to lack of equipment, as Quartermaster Ron Shambrook recalled:

> The biggest job was trying to get the base equipped to be able to manage a small number of people in defence of a

large area whilst the battalion was out. We then had to go and secure by fair or foul means switchboards, telephones; we got some .30 cal and .50 cal machine guns.[6]

It wasn't just the fighting gear that was in short supply, but also the very basics of life, such as food and shelter. As Ron explained:

> There was plenty of wire and pickets, that wasn't a problem. Tentage was the biggest problem because the pundits in Sydney said we would be able to take over the tents from 1 RAR, and of course when we got up there they had already had twelve months of good use. Anyway when we said the 1 RAR tents had rotted, they finished up coming up without the tent poles because they said the tent poles wouldn't have rotted, they wouldn't need them, and of course we never got the tent poles from 1 RAR. So there were lots of dramas in that respect. The food was interesting as well; at one stage there we were on frankfurters and corn for about two weeks. Lots and lots of fresh food was arriving, but we couldn't keep it in anything—we had no refrigerators.[7]

The 5 RAR group went back to Nui Dat in October 2005. To their surprise, it looked almost the same as it did in 1966, as it is now a fully-grown rubber plantation once more. As Peter Isaacs remarked, 'Apart from Luscombe Field, it did look almost as it did on the day that we got there.' On Operation Hardihood Captain Isaacs had 'flown in with the battalion of the 173rd Airborne and walked over Nui Dat hill before the Task Force [Headquarters] arrived'. Apart from 'fewer trees', he said, 'it didn't look that different'.

Peter looked around at a few decaying remains of the old base and observed:

> The stone pillars that used to mark the entrance to 1 ATF base on the Hoa Long side are still there. The remains of a command post bunker in the artillery regiment are still there too. Nui Dat hill has been partially excavated, but is certainly recognisable. Not quite so many trees as it had when I walked up it with the BHQ [Battalion Head-quarters] party of the 1/503rd [a US infantry battalion from 173rd Airborne Brigade], but the surrounding area is much the same as it probably was when a French Groupe Mobile was ambushed just to the west of the hill, by the Viet Minh in the early 1950s.[8]

The battalion's helicopter landing zone, known as 'Tiger Pad', is also still intact and became the obvious choice for holding a small, low-key and unobtrusive memorial service in which the 5 RAR group read out the names of those who had fallen on the battalion's first and second tours. They had a picnic lunch—and true to form it rained, turning the red lateritic soil to sticky red mud. They stood on the side of Nui Dat hill, which has been mined to a small extent in the search for high-grade pumice stone, and they took in the verdant green rice paddies, the multitudinous shades of green from crops like tapioca, rice, sweet potatoes, corn or maize and a host of vegetables. Cattle were being prodded along from one grazing spot to another by a young village boy, and the villagers were dotted among the green fields like punctuation marks, either harvesting or sowing fresh crops, wearing traditional black work clothes and bamboo hats.

The Warbies

When you are standing on the airstrip, or what is left of the crumbling tarmac of Luscombe Field, and look south-west you can see the distinctive line of hills known as the Nui Thi Vais. To the servicemen they were more commonly known as 'The Warbies'. Paul Greenhalgh gave the group the background to the naming of the hills:

> That all started back in Holsworthy. We built a mud map outside Delta Company headquarters about 10 feet by 10 feet and of course the biggest feature was the Nui Thi Vais. There was a popular tune at the time that included the lyrics, 'They say don't go on Warburton Mountain'. And there was a Private Warburton in Delta Company, and somebody put a sign up on the mud map that said, 'Don't go there Warby.' So when we as a company went to Viet Nam, we up on Nui Dat hill looked out onto the Nui Thi Vais so clearly. We called it the Warburtons—the Warbies—and that was used for the whole decade of Australian troops in Viet Nam. Sadly Private Warburton was killed; he was one of the four soldiers killed in the company.[9]

Ben Morris appreciated spending time at Nui Dat. 'Having the lunchbreak on the site was a lot better than being rushed in and out, which happened the first time I went there.' Although the authorities are not keen on visitors having memorial services, which is understandable, Ben felt that their simple service at Tiger Pad was important—as was 'just being there. Just standing and feeling the place.'[10]

Fred Pfitzner enjoyed being back in his old lines. After the lunchbreak, he wandered down to the area where he thought his lines would have been. He found it was:

> Pretty much as I remembered it. The rubber is back to about the same standard as it was when we were there, even though it is the second planting. There's no way I could have said precisely that's where my hoochie was or anything like that. But that wasn't important to me. Just to go back, look at the view, and say, 'Yep. I remember certain things that went on in there.' And move on.[11]

Peter Rogers was working with 161 Recce Squadron when he lived at Nui Dat. On his first trip back with his wife he recalled: 'I walked around Nui Dat and I showed Suzie where my hoochie was. I managed to find the area, even though new rubber had been planted in the area where it [once] was.' Peter took great delight in being able to share that memory with his wife. Being a pilot, he added: 'What I really wanted to do was hire a Cessna and fly around because that is the way I remember it, and to be able to see everything again.' However, there are no light fixed-wing aircraft for hire. Peter said ruefully, 'I could have hired a helicopter, but at $US1500 an hour, I thought that was a bit beyond our budget.'[12]

Today a large rubber factory sits beside the airstrip not far from where the refuelling farm was situated; across the other side of the strip is a kindergarten built by the Australian Veterans Vietnam Reconstruction Group.[13]

The Nui Dat medical fraternity

John Taske, Tony White and Ted Heffernan were all doctors serving in Nui Dat at the same time in 1966–67. They had all been at the School of Army Health together receiving their orientation training before they deployed to South Viet Nam. The men were attached to various elements within the Task Force such as 5 RAR, 1 Field Regiment and 6 RAR. While in country they had almost no opportunity to see each other owing to operational commitments, but towards the end of their tour they managed to gather together near John Taske's tent for a drink—or three—as John recalled:

> Ted thought of it. He stood up in his very expansive atti-
> tude ... and he said, 'Gentlemen, I call to order the first,
> last and only meeting of the Nui Dat Medical Association
> and in honour I will buy the first round.' And the gunners
> had some French pink champagne and so his first round
> was a bottle for each of us. So then we all had to buy a
> bottle in the round, so we ended up between the four of
> us drinking sixteen bottles of champagne.[14]

On the site of their serious imbibing almost 40 years earlier, the trio of medicos gathered again in October 2005 and cracked a bottle of champagne. They knew they were close to where they'd held their one and only meeting of the 'Nui Dat Medical Association'. As John explained, 'I was very close to the gates at Nui Dat—and to be able to find that spot and be within a few, oh, probably tens of metres of where I actually was, was a great thrill.'

Tony White was also happy with the re-enactment and being able to see his old lines again: 'It was a great, pleasant surprise . . . That was a great experience.'[15]

His son Rupert reported that Dr White had also experienced a sense of physical relief at the site: he 'had a leak where he reckoned the old pissaphone was'.[16] Tony later admitted to committing what he called a 'commemorative act' next to the former 5 RAR regimental aid post, where the latrine facility had been.

Restrictions at Nui Dat

When returning to Nui Dat, many veterans want to go back to where their old lines were located. Unfortunately this is not always possible: Nui Dat is now a military zone with the Australians' old nemesis—D 445 *Provincial Mobile Force Battalion*—billeted in the area where the 'Anzac lines' (2, 4 and 6 RAR) used to be on the eastern flank of the base. Consequently, veterans will not be allowed to enter the military restricted zone, but they can still go up onto Nui Dat hill and walk along the airstrip and drive around most of the old base area, which is now farmed extensively. A permit is required to enter the area, and unauthorised visitors will be escorted out, if not at gun point, then with some force.

Before the trip, Roger Wainwright was keen to 'go back and see my old platoon position' on the northern side of the airstrip. After his visit to Nui Dat Roger was elated. Grinning broadly, he said, 'I found it, and I didn't need a GPS to do it either.' He added:

I knew pretty well exactly where my tent was. I wandered around my platoon position; I knew how it was laid out and particularly the .50 cal bunker position that was down the front. And I went down there and had a look at that. And I knew from the fall of ground where it was.[17]

Reinforcing the need for veterans to have time to reflect during a battlefield visit, Roger remarked: 'I would have liked a little bit longer there. Just to have a little bit of time, you know, just to reflect about my mates.' Roger was responsible for drawing together the small ceremony at 'Tiger Pad' and shared his thoughts on what that meant to him:

That was special. And we did that purposely because when we came back from various operations and we'd lost people we'd have commemorative services with the whole battalion lined up around that square pad. So that's why we chose that position to do it. And at the same time to remember our comrades from the second tour of 5 RAR. We had 25 lost on each tour. So . . . as an association we weren't going to forget them.[18]

Veterans will find that returning to where they lived for a year will evoke a lot of memories. As Ron Shambrook said so succinctly, 'It was nostalgic.' Little things will shake the dust of time off the memory banks and images and thoughts will come flooding back. I found myself inwardly smiling at various things that started to return to the front of the brain, and often they were just trivial things—like the rubbish truck doing its rounds, and men playing volleyball between the rubber trees, and going in forlorn hope down to the Post Exchange to see if there were any reel-to-reel tape recorders left after the base wallahs and pogos had cleaned out the store. The latrines—rows of thunderboxes whose lids would lift when the 155 and 8-inch self-propelled American artillery let loose—pissaphones, sandbagging and gun pickets, mud, dust and duckboards.

Home, sweet home.

Chapter 5

OUTSIDE THE WIRE: PHUOC TUY

Travelling outside the wire throughout Phuoc Tuy is relatively simple. The arterials are all well marked and guides very rarely get geographically misplaced. I have even used a war-era map and been able to get from one side of the province to the other with little trouble. Most groups base themselves down at Vung Tau while they spend a couple of days touring the province. The areas they will normally visit are Nui Dat, The Horseshoe, the Memorial Cross site at Long Tan; they will also do a circuit around the mountains at the southern end of the province including the Long Hai Hills, and the Nui Thi Vai and Nui Dinh Mountains. If they have time, groups can also venture further afield to Xuyen Moc and do a circuit up to Binh Ba north of Nui Dat, and then motor west across the Hat Dich area and turn south back down past Long Son Island to Vung Tau.

Ba Ria–Vung Tau (Phuoc Tuy) Province

Situated about 40 kilometres south-east of the former Saigon, Phuoc Tuy Province—now known as Ba Ria–Vung Tau Province—was the area the Australian Task Force were responsible for as part of the Allied effort against the Viet Cong. The province covered approximately 2500 square kilometres, consisting of coastal plains with sand dunes to the south, the Mekong River Delta with mangroves and swamps in the south-west, and three isolated jungle-covered mountain groups to the south-east, with Ba Ria as its capital. The province was chosen for a number of reasons. It was strategically important as it contained the port facility of Vung Tau where Australian logistics could be brought ashore, and the vital Route 15 arterial road between the port and Saigon. Although heavily controlled by the Viet Cong, the province could also be contained using Australian counter-revolutionary warfare techniques, and the terrain—mostly flat and covered in jungle—suited the Australian forces and their military structure for operations.

Phuoc Tuy Province was an operational backwater compared to the northern provinces of South Viet Nam near the demilitarised zone (DMZ) on the 17th Parallel border. However, it harboured fewer suspected enemy than the regions to the north, and was an area where the Task Force could manage its own military affairs to a certain degree and work in accordance with Australian Army doctrine and tactical procedures.

The province has changed dramatically since the war ended. Returning veterans will notice the changes to the village structures, the widened and bitumened roads—some of which are now toll roads—and the overall increase in village and population density. They will also have to buy new maps as many of the road and street designations have changed—and in many cases throughout Viet Nam, towns have also been renamed, usually to honour a local war hero or represent a Communist victory.

Once the veteran enters the old province, whether by road down from Ho Chi Minh City, or by the much-preferred hydrofoil ferry down the Song Sai Gon (Saigon River), things will begin to look familiar, and memories will start flooding back. The major geographical features have not changed, although since 1993 the vegetation on top of the Nui Thi Vais has started to regrow after decades of being barren as a result of defoliant spraying.

Vung Tau

The first place many veterans saw in the province if they came by sea aboard HMAS *Sydney*—the converted aircraft carrier that operated as a troopship and stores carrier—was the port and resort city of Vung Tau, about 130 kilometres south-east of Ho Chi Minh City. The wreck of a ship was prominent at Cap St Jacques, but it has long since gone to the scrap-metal yards. The city is once again a seaside resort town, and attracts flocks of residents from Ho Chi Minh City on weekends, especially young courting couples on motorcycles.

During the war, when the *Sydney* arrived in the port the soldiers were most often ferried ashore by American Army Chinook helicopters. For most Australians it was the first time they had ever seen one of these huge machines— which one American compatriot once described most colourfully as 'two palm trees fuckin' in a bucket'—let alone fly in one. Once on board, the American crewmen would ensure that the soldiers' rifles were pointed down towards the floor so that an accidental discharge didn't take out the vital hydraulics that kept those two 'palm trees' operating. Bill Kromwyk recalled his maiden flight in one of the huge noisy machines:

> I just remember looking around at everybody's faces and—with the exception of Bob [Bettany]—how green and bewildered they looked. It was a whole new experience; here we are in Viet Nam. And then I looked at the American gunners on the doors and the pilots—there were about five crew—and they were sort of hardened and had a laid-back sort of look. And I thought, 'My God, we certainly are green compared to these guys. Just look at them.' I felt like a really green soldier.[1]

Vung Tau was a relatively secure area; there was little direct threat from the Viet Cong by day, and only occasionally by night. Any enemy activity was usually in the form of sporadic rocket attacks or small-scale ground attacks on Regional Force or Popular Force outposts in the local area.[2]

Mortarman Private Garry Heskett was flown ashore in a Chinook and said he experienced feelings of dread, admitting he had 'a feeling of slight nervousness, antici-pation and being super-alert, believing that the enemy were hiding behind every bush and tree'.[3]

Bill Kromwyk was doing his National Service with 6 RAR on their second tour of duty in 1969–70, and came ashore from the HMAS *Sydney* by other means:

> We were anchored off Vung Tau and then the landing craft came and got us. We went from there in the landing

craft to land on Vung Tau. We climbed down into the landing craft and we couldn't see anything, all we knew was that we were heading towards Vung Tau and didn't know what to expect. We were told that probably nothing will happen but, just in case, be careful. I don't know if we even had any ammunition! Of course nothing happened. I always remember the big ramp coming down and there were all these officers standing there waiting for us. There was no enemy. So we piled off and we had to march to the airstrip, and the [RAAF] Caribous took us to Nui Dat.[4]

When 5 RAR first arrived in country in 1966 they were to be part of the 1 ATF. The battalion main body (about 700 men) was sent down to the sand dunes of Back Beach to acclimatise and prepare for Operation Hardihood, which was to be conducted in close coordination with American units to secure the Task Force base area.[5] The sand dunes were hot, windswept and not at all inviting. There was a total lack of facilities and the equipment the soldiers needed to prepare for their immediate task.

Captain Peter Isaacs stood on what is now a Viet Cong martyrs' monument—where once the 1st Australian Logistic Support Group (1 ALSG) Officers' Mess stood—and looked down at the four-lane toll road leading to Ba Ria, and several hotel resorts under construction near the beach. He commented, 'I think it looks ghastly.'[6] Not everyone has that same opinion and many are glad to see the area forging ahead, fuelled in part by massive off-shore oil and gas exploration projects that are now bringing energy resources and wealth into the area. Peter reflected:

I've wandered around the world since those days and the development that's gone on is typical of development that goes on which is unplanned, haphazard. Some of the buildings are very good, and I certainly applaud the Vietnamese [for] the gardens that they have developed and so on. But Back Beach? Well, it was a stretch of sand, and it was as I expected it would be.[7]

Paul Greenhalgh recalled his most vivid memory of Vung Tau as:

Standing on the sand at the ALSG at Vung Tau ... talking to the soldiers before Operation Hardihood. We flew in by choppers from Vung Tau and I remember going on a bit like a football coach, geeing them up and saying, 'Here we go, here we go.' And then there was a short [chopper] flight up to what was the Nui Dat area and landing. It was on; we were away.[8]

During their tour of duty soldiers would be given a few days' R&C leave at Vung Tau. This was usually granted about six times during a one-year tour, if you were lucky, and was designed to refresh soldiers. Groups of about 100 or more could be accommodated at a time, and when the 1 ALSG rest centre was established at Back Beach it was called the Peter Badcoe Club after the posthumously decorated Victoria Cross winner from the AATTV. Soldiers were then billeted in a hostel in town, which was named 'The Flags' on account of Allied nations' flags decorating the opposite street. The men were free for about 48 hours to visit the town dressed in civilian attire, and went unarmed—but also forewarned that the greatest danger they now faced was not the VC but VD. There were about 3000 bar girls plying their trade, and sexually transmitted diseases were prevalent; it was an offence if a soldier failed to take precautions and became a casualty.

So, it was a case of taking it easy and relaxing by swimming, drinking, boating, drinking, dining out and drinking, and occasionally taking in the cultural delights of the town such as bars, saloons and hotels. The Military Police were kept busy and generally most of the soldiery who went to Vung Tau had a good time—if they could remember it. The officers were billeted at the Grand Hotel, which sat on Front Beach facing the South China Sea and had a luxurious beer garden, a reasonable restaurant and of course the obligatory dimly lit bar, where exorbitantly priced drinks were dispensed by hostesses who insisted on being bought a 'Saigon tea', which was a method of extracting good money for worthless coloured water.

A popular ditty that circulated at the time has now re-emerged on souvenir items ranging from T-shirts to stubby coolers, which are boldly emblazoned with versions of these words:

> Uc Dai Loi, he cheap Charlie,
> He no buy me Saigon tea,
> Saigon tea cost many many pee*
> Uc Dai Loi, he cheap Charlie
> (* for piastre—the local currency during the war)

Bill Kromwyk was asked if he remembered his visit to Vung Tau on R&C leave and he replied, '. . . sort of'. On his first visit back in 2001, Bill stayed in a hotel and walked around the town. 'But it all looked different you know, I couldn't quite recognise much of it—just around near the Grand [Hotel], I thought I remembered a little bit around there.'9

Ben Morris had reasons for not liking the town when he went down there on R&C leave with his platoon. The staunch Catholic explained:

> To me Vung Tau was the Forbidden City. It was the place I didn't really like going. I hated taking soldiers there on R&C because the bastards would all piss off. They'd all be in the out of bounds area and there was not much you could do about it ... And invariably there were the one or two that you had to find and no-one in the world loves going back to Nui Dat to face the CO, missing a Digger or two.10

Ben has been back to Viet Nam three times now and has travelled from one end to the other. Of the modern Vung Tau he said:

> Vung Tau is like a lot of Viet Nam. It's moved on. It's become cleaner. For a Communist country they believe in a lot of capitalism. I really am intrigued by the fact that here we are in a country that's supposed to be Communist, and it's raw capitalism.11

Fred Pfitzner was based in Nui Dat and only visited Vung Tau a few times during his tour of duty. Asked whether he was disappointed in the changes and being unable to recognise places, Fred replied, 'Not at all. I would have been disappointed not to have seen great change.'12

Aviator Peter Rogers also went around town looking for landmarks and explained:

> We had a sister unit in Vung Tau, the 54th Aviation Company, and they used to do maintenance for us, and if we went to Vung Tau we would stay with them. I went looking for their place and it was hopeless because the whole of Vung Tau has changed so much. I was also amazed at how big Ba Ria had become, monstrous.[13]

Ron Shambrook recalled his own reaction to visiting Vung Tau after 40 years.

> When I first saw Vung Tau there was virtually nothing on those sand dunes, and now there's high-rise resorts and apartments. In our tour [1966–67] we didn't have the Badcoe Club complex and the swimming pool and ALSG, and no more permanent accommodation than tents. Towards the end of our tour, my company—Charlie Company—was given the task of going down and setting up some tents near the beach so we could cycle people through to help their health.[14]

When the 5 RAR pilgrims returned to Vung Tau in 2005 they arrived on the hydrofoil ferry service from Ho Chi Minh City. John Taske recalled his reaction as they entered the port:

> It brought back a lot of memories. That was the view that I got because I came up on the HMAS *Sydney* with Charlie Company. And Back Beach—it was a disappointment from the point of view that it looked absolutely nothing like when we first arrived because all it was was

just undulating sand hills—it was just tents among the sand dunes. And then when the monsoons came, it all got flooded out and then they had to level it and start again. But it was nothing like what I expected. But it's beautiful; I'm delighted to see it develop.[15]

Roger Wainwright had the honour of commanding the first rifle platoon into the Back Beach area in 1966, which was then a mass—and mess—of empty sand hills. Roger was to a large extent the senior tactical person in the area, and here he recounts his journey after landing at Tan Son Nhut:

We got into a C-123 [Provider] and flew down to Vung Tau airstrip . . . We were put into the back of a cattle truck and went through what were essentially sand hills to Back Beach. There was no population around; we were going through winding little sand hills in that area. We spent the next couple of days essentially putting up [fencing] wire for the rest of the battalion so they could put up their hoochies. I was just racing around making sure the area was secure.[16]

The 5th Battalion did some refresher training as well as the normal acclimatisation runs and physical training to maintain fitness. 'We were the only battalion that used Back Beach as a firing range, firing mortars and RCLs [recoilless rifles] and small arms out to sea at a few floating targets dumped out there by a boat.'[17] It was far from pleasant— 'stinking hot and no shade, in the full sun on the sand, and problems with weapons'.

Asked how he felt when he was approaching Vung Tau again, Roger replied: 'Coming down the river on the hydrofoil and just seeing Cap Saint Jacques and Little Hill and Big Hill in the background sort of gives you a few goose bumps and things like that.'[18]

In 1966 the 5 RAR officers took a group photo at Back Beach, and when the pilgrimage group regathered there in 2005 they did not let the moment pass unrecorded. Recreating situations such as group photos (and the Nui Dat medical fraternity champagne toast) can provide lasting memories that allow the veteran to assess the passing of time and place their past service in perspective.

The pièce de résistance, however, was saved for when the group assembled for dinner one night in Vung Tau, dressed resplendently in slacks, shirts and gold battalion cravats. Did they look out of place in Vung Tau? Absolutely. Did they care? Absolutely not. The party then had a group dinner at a local restaurant owned by expatriate Australian Alan Davis and his Vietnamese wife Anh, during which Tony White showed a compilation video from all his 8-mm film that he took during his tour of duty in Viet Nam. It created a terrific atmosphere—and the bar owner's wife, who came from near Binh Ba, recalled some of the incidents on the film footage and said it brought tears to her eyes when she recognised the Army doctors doing their Medcaps. It was a memorable evening all round.

Long Son Island

Not far north up the road from the port city of Vung Tau is Long Son Island. The island is about seven kilometres long from east to west, three kilometres wide from north to south, with a large hilly complex on the eastern end. During the war it was totally isolated, except by boat; today a causeway at the eastern end connects the island to the mainland. Near the causeway is a village, and a hamlet is located at the far western end. Apart from some industrial estate development near the causeway, the island has not changed very dramatically since 5 RAR conducted Operation Hayman between 8 and 12 November 1966, a search and clear operation designed to flush any lurking enemy out of the hilly, scrubby areas into the more open lowland areas where they could more easily be rounded up. During the operation, Australian SAS patrols stood by in inflatable boats to intercept enemy soldiers fleeing the sweep. The insertion was not without incident, as Ron Shambrook recalled:

> We flew into the top of this hill and it was a marginal LZ because the gradient of this hill was very poor; too steep. And anyway the first four choppers landed and they indicated that they were getting some small arms fire. I came in in the second group of four, and so our attention to detail was good at that stage, because nothing rivets your attention more than a little bit of lead flying through the air, but there was none when we landed. Anyway the fourth lift came in and one of the pilots over-corrected and thrashed the plane to bits by running the rotors into the hill. I thought we were being mortared; it made an awful lot of noise and I didn't know what was happening there for a moment.[19]

In 2005, the 5 RAR group returned to Long Son Island and after some good observation and deduction were able to determine which helicopter pad they had flown into halfway up the hillside—it was virtually unchanged. Having kept their operational maps, the veteran infantrymen were able to locate almost exactly where they had fought and where various incidents occurred. Ted Heffernan had conducted a Medcap in the local village on Long Son Island, and located a monastery close to where he had helped the villagers during the offensive operations being conducted about two kilometres away. Wandering around the small village, Ted was able to recognise buildings and the area where he had worked during Operation Hayman. When he returned to the group he was beaming from ear to ear and telling all and sundry what he had found. The tour bus filled with smiles.

The Horseshoe

The Horseshoe was an almost circular hill about eight kilometres south-east of Nui Dat—which was still within artillery range—and less than one kilometre north of a large village called Dat Do. It was a prominent feature that allowed observation over a large area of the flat countryside: with binoculars it was possible to see almost anything that moved to the east of Dat Do village, making it an excellent vantage point and information-gathering site.

A permanent fire support base was established on The Horseshoe, normally comprising a rifle company, a section or more of 81-mm mortars and three armoured personnel carriers (APCs), providing a ready reaction force to rapidly assist any troops in trouble or to set up quick roadblocks to intercept suspicious traffic. It was also well defended with Claymore mines, barbed wire and fighting bays dug into the rocky soil.

The Horseshoe was established in 1967 by a rifle company from 5 RAR and commanded by Paul Greenhalgh, whose previous company had been positioned on top of Nui Dat hill. Paul was a rare breed—an unmarried major—but had become engaged to future wife Wendy, who was a school teacher working at RMC Duntroon teaching dependants' kids. He didn't especially relish being sent to establish the fire support base at The Horseshoe—and it wasn't always known by that name, as Paul explained:

> Well actually the Horseshoe feature wasn't given a name when we were sent out there. It was just a volcanic crater—but I will say it now, being a student of military history, General Christian de Castries had named all of his outposts [at Dien Bien Phu] after his mistresses. I called it Fort Wendy.[20]

But digging into the hard granite rock was not easy and before long expletives were being directed at the name of the outpost. Paul decided that he wouldn't have his fiancée's name slurred anymore and so it became known as The Horseshoe. In 2005, the woman after whom this rocky outcrop had once been named stood next to the feature and remarked modestly about how she felt upon finally seeing it:

I'm glad actually it [the name] only lasted two days. It would have been quite weird to have a place in Viet Nam named after you . . . It was great that Paul had it for two days, but it was much better that it went on to be called The Horseshoe.[21]

Fred Pfitzner, who bounced from one company to another filling in shortfalls as a company second-in-command (2IC)—at one stage he was in Charlie Company for only 24 hours before being reassigned—took up the story of The Horseshoe:

I became known as 'Fred the Wandering Jew'. I didn't know where they were going to send me and the next thing they said was, 'Well we are building The Horseshoe, the 2IC has gone off home on the advance party and you are it.' So I went and did that with Paul Greenhalgh and we built The Horseshoe. That was good; I enjoyed my time in Delta Company.[22]

On my last four trips, including the 2005 5 RAR pilgrimage, I have been unable to gain access to The Horseshoe owing to blasting at what is now a quarry site. The northern half of the feature has been dug out, and if quarrying continues at the present rate, within five years the hill will most probably be unrecognisable to veterans.

An Nhut

For the 5 RAR group one of the principal reasons for coming on the pilgrimage was to return to the scene of a dreadful mine incident that occurred during Operation Beaumauris between 12 and 14 February 1967. A cordon and search was being conducted of the hamlet of An Nhut, which is ten kilometres east of Ba Ria. Charlie Company had its headquarters decimated when the OC, Major Don Bourne, the company 2IC Captain Bob Milligan and the artillery forward observer Captain Peter Williams were all killed. Six other soldiers were wounded by the blast. The battalion had only nine weeks to go before they returned to Australia.

The village of An Nhut has only grown a little since the war, and the rice-paddy area where the mine incident occurred is still basically as it was 40 years ago. Roger Wainwright had a photograph that was taken just before the explosion, and when his group went to the site in 2005 they were able to stand within five metres of where those men were killed. In a moving tribute, Roger laid a floral offering at the spot. Under a cloudless sky in searing heat everyone observed a few minutes' silence to remember those who lost their lives or were wounded on that terrible day.

Roger was a platoon commander in the ill-fated Charlie Company. Determined to get to An Nhut, he had ensured that the tour company could and would take his group there during their pilgrimage. He explained why it was so important to him and the others:

It was a significant moment in our company as well as the battalion. To lose three people like that—and let's not forget the six wounded, of which a couple had to come home. I got to know the family, the widow of Don Bourne and his four children. I'd phoned them just about a month ago [September 2005] and spoke to one of the sons and said I was coming over here, and asked would you like us to lay something on the spot if we could find it. And they said to me, 'If you can just take a photograph of the position.' We achieved that. And apart from the rice paddies being green as against dry and brown at the time, it's exactly the same shot.[23]

There are moments during pilgrimages when incidents like An Nhut will sweep over veterans and create a melancholy. It cannot be avoided, nor should it be. John Taske was a good friend of Charlie Company's 2IC Bob Milligan, and sadly recalled:

I went over to his tent [the night before] and he was telling me all about how he'd finally made up his mind—coming up on the ship he'd kept talking about this girl and whether he should get married and stuff like that. And then he'd told me that he was getting engaged and he was just so full of joy at going home. And then, to hear a couple of days later that he'd bought it, was pretty sad.[24]

The Long Hai Hills

The Long Hai Hills are a cluster of relatively high hills in the south-eastern corner of Ba Ria–Vung Tau Province, sitting about twenty kilometres to the south of the 1 ATF base at Nui Dat and running down to the coast. During the war, with its thick vegetation and steep slopes strewn with granite boulders, it was a formidable piece of terrain that was easy to defend and very difficult to attack. It was an ideal sanctuary as the approaches were open and flat, and any encroaching movement could be easily detected, especially in the dry season. The massive boulders and natural caves and crevices afforded excellent concealment and protection from direct and indirect fire.

The Long Hai Hills were never a good place to get to, as Paul Greenhalgh recalled: 'You were always buggered! You were looking at your toes as you were climbing hills. Fatigue when we got up to the top ... It was extremely wearying and tiresome.'[25]

The Long Hai Hills were also known as the Minh Dam Secret Zone, after a Viet Minh base there named after the local guerrilla leader, Minh, and his deputy, Dam. The Secret Zone had been a guerrilla stronghold since the First Indochina War and remained active against ARVN and Australian troops during the entire Viet Nam War. It was never conquered and was considered a notorious 'badland' as it was difficult to manoeuvre, and mines and booby traps were prolific. Whenever enemy troops needed a place to rest, refit or recover they would use the Minh Dam Secret Zone as their sanctuary.

Derrill De Heer had to work down in the 'badlands' on occasion and sometimes flew over them when he was working the Psyops Unit. When asked what made him apprehensive he responded emphatically, 'Flying over the Long Hai broadcasting or dropping leaflets from a low height. I was shot at a number of times. The aircraft was not allowed to retaliate as we wanted them to surrender.'[26]

Peter Isaacs didn't relish working in the area either, adding: 'The Long Hai Hills had bad memories for us at the end of our tour.'[27] As they did for rifleman Bill Kromwyk: '6 RAR took a lot of casualties there actually. Yes that always worried me, I used to hate being in that area.'[28]

Fred Pfitzner was intrigued by his visit to the Long Hais in 2005:

> Getting up into that area I found quite fascinating because every time we'd try to get up there we got bloodied. No matter whether it was a unit like 5 RAR on its first tour, or 4 RAR on its last. If you went up there you were going to get clobbered. So when you get up into it you can see what a fiendishly difficult area it would have been to get into and maintain any sort of presence.[29]

Most tour groups visiting the province are offered the option of going up into the Long Hai Hills. A lookout right on the eastern tip of the range offers spectacular views up and down the coast, and near the lookout is a small monastery that is home to Cao Dai monks. There is also a small museum and cafe run by an ex-D 445 *Battalion* lieutenant, Hoang Ngan, which has been operating for approximately eight years.

The area has allegedly been cleared of mines and booby traps, but one should nevertheless exercise caution and avoid moving off the well-defined tracks. The Long Hais had ordnance of all kinds dumped on it during both Indochina wars, and there are undoubtedly still many undiscovered and unexploded munitions in the hills. When the natural gas pipeline was being laid through supposedly cleared areas several years ago, in excess of 100 unexploded ordnance items were reportedly found.

I have visited the area on three occasions and each time former Lieutenant Hoang welcomed me as a comrade in arms. It can be disconcerting at first to stand in front of a former foe and shake his hand knowing that at one stage you were both possibly trying to kill each other. However, the warmth and hospitality shown by former enemy soldiers is not uncommon, and Australian soldiers are met with open arms and with disarming frankness.

The 5 RAR pilgrimage group had not encountered a former Viet Cong soldier before, and afterwards were individually asked how they felt about meeting Mr Hoang. Ben Morris replied simply, 'That's the time the hating stopped. Just meeting him; he's a human being . . . He welcomed us.' Of the hundreds of Viet Nam veterans that I've spoken to over the last three decades, very few hold or feel any 'hatred' towards their former foe. Fred Pfitzner put it thus:

> They were doing what they had to do, and we were doing what we had to do. I mean, there's a universal brotherhood of infantry. You all suffer the same way. And how they got in there [to the Long Hais] with large bodies of troops and managed to secure them away from observation, the air strikes, and artillery. How they managed to feed and water them. How they managed to fix them up medically when they needed it. I've got nothing but admiration for them. And even at the time, I thought, you know, these blokes are no dills. They know what they're doing.[30]

Roger Wainwright was similarly philosophical. 'I think we've got to respect what our foes were doing at the time,' he remarked. After reflecting that both he and Mr Hoang had been of the same rank, he added:

> I think the fact is that war overall is a nasty thing, and the suffering occurs to both sides. And to meet them in more friendly circumstances all those years later is interesting. And, you can't say there is any malice remaining in this day and age. It was great to meet him. I would have liked to have had a longer chat with him.[31]

As a doctor, Tony White didn't physically go up into the Long Hais during the war, but certainly had to deal with the result of Allied operations in the foothills. 'My main link with the area was the Operation Renmark mine incident, and of course we couldn't get within cooee of that.'[32] Operation Renmark was conducted in the Long Hai Hills between 18 and 22 February 1967, and 22 February was another black day for the 5th Battalion. Three infantry soldiers and two cavalry crewmen were killed, and another nine men were wounded, when their armoured personnel carrier ran over a mine most probably constructed from a large unexploded aerial bomb. Four Platoon, commanded by Lieutenant John Carruthers, was leading a mounted advance and had struck the mine.

During the immediate commotion and commencement of the casualty evacuation phase and reorganisation of the company, an M-16 'Jumping Jack' mine was triggered—and within four minutes of the initial incident many more men were seriously wounded. Captain Tony

White was the RMO of 5 RAR and was flown in by Sioux helicopter, to be greeted with an atmosphere of deep shock and fear. Captain Peter Isaacs notified Task Force Headquarters and within minutes an Iroquois Dustoff chopper was overhead, awaiting the preparation of a landing zone at the point of the explosions. The scene was horrendous, with a total of 31 wounded.

Another excruciating problem for Tony was determining who would be treated first of the large group of casualties, several of whom were in danger of imminent death. Fortunately the 36th US Evacuation Hospital at Vung Tau was only five minutes away by Iroquois, and the more severely wounded cases were on operating tables within 25 minutes of being wounded. Major Bruce McQualter was still just conscious when Tony arrived, and urged him to treat the 4 Platoon casualties first. Shortly afterwards Bruce lost consciousness. Lieutenant Carruthers was also seriously wounded, and despite severe head and body injuries, each man held on to life with great tenacity. Lieutenant Carruthers died on 24 February, and Major McQualter at 5 a.m. on 5 March.[33]

Even after having to deal with the incredible trauma and horrific injuries inflicted by the former enemy, Tony White expressed these feelings after meeting Mr Hoang:

No ill feelings at all. No, I feel that was then. He was a 17-year-old who went in there and he was defending his country. We were on our side doing our duty, and it just highlighted the absurdity of the whole exercise. And many deaths and a lot of people knocked around mentally and physically.[34]

Binh Ba

Binh Ba, seven kilometres north of Nui Dat, was—and still is today—a rubber plantation workers' village and very picturesque. The houses are built in orderly rows, and most have concrete walls, tiled roofs, and wooden doors and window shutters. While there are trees and shrubs between and at the rear of houses, the front is usually well mown. It has a properly laid out road system, and the eastern edge of the village is next to the former Route 2 roadway.

This village was cordoned and searched by 5 RAR very early in their tour of duty, and many following battalions based their modus operandi on how 5 RAR went about their business. Roger Wainwright recalled that first cordon of the village and what he remembered most:

> I suppose the approach to it by night into the position as we did with all of those cordons. It was pretty much the very first one that we did, and of the absolute vital necessity of linking up at night time with other companies so that you don't have clashes with other platoons. And walking at night with toggle ropes.[35]

Today the village has grown somewhat, but is still essentially a community of local rubber plantation workers. Entry is restricted at times—on my last two visits I have been denied access to the village, but I have not been able to ascertain exactly why. The day the 5 RAR group arrived, entry was again restricted and it was bucketing rain. The group was not given a permit to enter the area from the Vietnamese government. Battle sites are declared 'sensitive areas' and permits must be obtained through the government tourist agencies or arrest and detention can result. People were allowed off the bus and looked across at the village. The veterans peered through the pelting tropical downpour at where they had once formed a perimeter around the village and flushed out dozens of Viet Cong soldiers and sympathisers. Adjutant and assistant operations officer Peter Isaacs commented ruefully, 'Binh Ba was unrecognisable apart from the water tower, and the airstrip is invisible from the road. There was no sign of the Regional Forces post we constructed.'[36]

Roger Wainwright was also disappointed he couldn't get into the village in 2005 because, 'After we did the initial cordon and search of Binh Ba, our company lived there for almost two months, and that is probably why we never finished digging in at Nui Dat.'[37]

Aviator Peter Rogers was also interested in visiting the village because he had been involved in the Battle at Binh Ba as part of Operation Hammer from 6 to 8 June 1969. 'It was a colossal stoush while I was there,' he reflected.[38] The road heading north up from the old Task Force base at Nui Dat was once an arterial road between isolated villages, right up to the next province capital of Bien Hoa. But since the war, the growth of the populated areas has been staggering. As Peter observed, 'I couldn't recognise the place. It is all ribbon development now.' Peter was saddened that he couldn't identify where the former airstrip had been located, north-west of Binh Ba, because two aviator friends were shot down and killed near there just after he finished his tour of duty.[39]

The tour group travelled from Binh Ba west across the area that was formerly known to Australians as the Hat Dich region. During the war it was a large tract of primary and secondary jungle; now a highway runs through it, supporting ribbon development, small towns, coffee and pepper plantations and market gardens. Fred Pfitzner said he couldn't believe it: 'I was gobsmacked at the development—it is bloody good to see it.'[40]

Xuyen Moc

Twenty kilometres due east of the Nui Dat base, but some 35 kilometres by gravel road, was the town of Xuyen Moc (pronounced 'Swen Mok'). It was a settlement that swelled from a rapid influx of Catholics who left North Viet Nam once the country had been divided in 1954.[41]

During the American War, the isolated town was subjected to constant harassment by the Viet Cong, who felt secure in attacking the local populace given the long reaction time required to deploy a large combat force to restore order and repel their forays. The road leading out to the town via the provincial capital of Ba Ria and the district capital of Long Dien was often mined, and subject to frequent motor vehicle ambushes. In 1966, 5 RAR was given the task of clearing the road and establishing a presence in Xuyen Moc. As Fred Pfitzner observed on the logistics of even getting there, 'To actually have got out to Xuyen Moc required a special operation every time it was ever done.'[42] After the war, the resettled North Vietnamese

Catholics paid the price for not buckling to Viet Cong pressure: the town was the very last in the province to receive electricity.

Dr Ted Heffernan conducted Medcaps at Xuyen Moc, and when he returned in 2005 he was absolutely thrilled to see the town and the people again. When the group alighted from their bus near a large Catholic school at Binh Gia they were mobbed by young children in bright blue school uniforms. Chaos reigned as the school kids gathered around, and some were rather bemused when staring at the heavily scarred, one-legged and black-eye-patched Peter Isaacs, who replied rather earnestly to an enquiry from an inquisitive child that he was in fact a pirate. Show and tell would have been something to eavesdrop on the next day.

Wendy Greenhalgh participated in a romp with several tour members and dozens of school kids and said later, 'Everybody was so happy—and I thought, God, why couldn't it always have been like that?'[43]

Chapter 6

LONG TAN: THE CROSS

The Long Tan Memorial Cross was first erected on the site of the massive battle in the Long Tan rubber plantation not far from the Nui Dat base during 6 RAR's second tour of duty, with serving battle survivors of Delta Company—the rifle company involved in that bitter encounter—in attendance. The Cross has become the focal point of Australian pilgrimages to Viet Nam for one simple reason. While battlefield pilgrimages have traditionally focused on visits to the cemeteries of war dead, in Viet Nam no Australians are buried in war cemeteries—it was the first overseas conflict in which most Australian dead were brought home for burial. A small number (24) of Australian dead from Viet Nam lie in the Australian section of the British War Cemetery in Terendak, Malaysia, and one serviceman in the Kranji Military Cemetery in Singapore, but that vital link with the past is not present in Viet Nam itself. The Long Tan Cross has come to represent the men killed in South Viet Nam, and is one of only two foreign monuments to the dead allowed in Viet Nam (the other is to the French at Dien Bien Phu). Veterans are permitted to visit the area in small numbers to pay tribute not only to the Long Tan dead, but to all veterans killed and injured during the war.

An escort by police and special permits are required to enter the Long Tan rubber plantation and Long Tan Memorial Cross area. Visitors need to travel up Route 764 towards Binh Ba and turn off onto Route 766, or if coming from the west turn off the Dat Do–Long Phuoc road and head north-east to the battle site past The Horseshoe to the rebuilt Long Tan village. Turn north near the signpost reading 'Long Khanh 59 km', then turn north into the battle site. Groups will have to stop at the police post in Long Tan village, where the bronze plaque that adorns the Cross is kept in safekeeping for placing. A small bus can take you almost right into the area, then it's a short 200-metre walk to the Cross.

As historian Elizabeth Stewart notes, 'The area has become sacred ground, and many comment on the eerie nature of the place. Few words are spoken in the simple ceremonies held there, but few visitors leave the area dry-eyed.'[1] The site has not always been in its present condition; it was previously a cornfield and tapioca patch. A decade ago, rubber was planted and the area is now almost as it was when Delta Company began patrolling through the area on that fateful, stormy afternoon of 18 August 1966.

While a visit to the Long Tan Cross provides a cathartic and emotional highlight for many pilgrims, another highlight involves meeting former enemy. In informal meetings—often with former members of the Viet Cong D 445 *Battalion*—veterans from both sides drink a toast and recognise in each other a common struggle with a difficult war legacy. Realising that their former enemies were simply soldiers doing a job, just as they were, is an important step for Australian veterans coming to terms with their past actions. They are often heartened, as well, by former South Vietnamese who thank the Australians for their efforts on their behalf, and for the public works they carried out, which helped improve lives during and after the war.

Tour leader Garry Adams believes the Long Tan battle-field is the main point of pilgrimage for most Australian veterans. Interestingly, however, it took until November 2006 for an Australian Prime Minister (John Howard) to visit what has become almost hallowed ground for Australian and New Zealand veterans of the war.

The visit to Long Tan is always an emotional experi-ence, especially for veterans or next of kin. Private Steve Campling was a National Serviceman who served with 6 RAR between September 1969 and May 1970 on its second tour of duty. He reflected on why the Long Tan Cross has such a special significance for him:

> The trip back to the Long Tan Memorial was one of the most moving experiences of my life. Being back in the rubber just brought back so many memories. To think how those fellows went through what they did is just totally unbelievable. And probably more moving for me also, because the 18th of August is my birthday and when the Cross was dedicated on 18 August 1969, I was here, and had my 21st birthday.[2]

Corporal Bob Hansford was 22 years old and a RAEME mechanic when he toured with 161 Independent Recce Flight in 1968–69. He visited Long Tan in 2002.

It was really eerie: . . . it just had a feeling about the place. It was very quiet. It must be hard for some of these other guys [in the tour group] too because they are mainly infantry, so they would have a much closer tie to it than myself.[3]

In 2002, Gail Campling visited the battlefield site with her husband Steve, in a tour group of which I was also a member. Afterwards, she confessed: 'I was extremely moved. I would have liked to have just sat there and meditated and tried to absorb all the feelings that I knew were there; all the pain and the suffering.'[4] Several years later I asked Gail to recount the most emotional experience from that trip and she said, 'The most moving highlight for me was at Long Tan hearing your version of those events. I almost felt I was there seeing it all unfold before my eyes.'[5]

For veterans who were in South Viet Nam when the battle took place, returning to the site is charged with memories and emotions. Paul Greenhalgh was commanding Delta Company 5 RAR and recalled the morning of the battle and subsequent events:

We were called back from Operation Holsworthy earlier because the Task Force had been mortared the night before. We were sitting up on [Nui Dat] hill and I must say we were starting to have our 'let down' beers, and the urgency of the mortaring of the base hadn't really got through to us—and [then] the guns started firing and of course that was the beginning of Long Tan or Operation Smithfield. The guns were firing from just down the bottom, all hell was going on, and then we finally twigged to what was happening. We closed the boozer and then I got a warning order to be ready at about 9 or 10 o'clock, as a company from 5 RAR under command 6 RAR, to go and supplement 6 RAR. Anyway we got cleaned up and stood by and just waited, and then we finally got marching orders to move at first light the next morning. We actually went out under command 6 RAR. We landed at the battle site, got orders from the CO 6 RAR, and we were the first company that went through the left-hand side of the battlefield in a clearing operation.[6]

On his visit in 2005, Paul was able to relate his experiences on that dreadful morning of moving through what battle veteran Bob Buick described as a 'charnel house'.[7] Paul recalled 'the smell and the cordite and the sheer destruction of the trees and the bodies that lay everywhere'. When asked what he most remembered about the battle site, Paul replied, 'It was total awe at the extent of the whole thing. I was talking to Harry Smith as we arrived and he just rolled his eyes and said, "I am lucky to be here, Paul." '[8]

Ron Shambrook was working as quartermaster of 5 RAR when the battle erupted. He vividly remembers the night before and then the day of the battle:

We had been mortared the night before and that took our attention, and also showed some inadequacies, because we had arrived there in May about three days before the wet season had cut in and so none of our overhead protection was in place and most of the holes [fighting pits] had a couple of feet of water in them. So when we were mortared that night it was a damp activity [chuckles]. During the battle, one could hear the enormous amount of artillery that was being fired. So I listened on the radio the whole time to 6 RAR and it was a very interesting day.[9]

Back at the Nui Dat base, Dr Ted Heffernan was kept busy treating soldiers who had been wounded during the battle and evacuated during the night. Ted reflected on that incredible battle from the perspective of one charged with putting soldiers back together again: 'That was the biggest thing that happened while we were here. We thought at the time that it was incredibly lucky the way it panned out. And looking back on it, it was.'[10]

Another doctor, John Taske, was serving with 1 Field Regiment, RAA. Returning to the battle site was significant for him because:

I was with the guns at the time and saw that side of it. I never saw the battlefield at all, and although I would have liked to have gone out there the next day and seen it, we weren't allowed to. So I had never ever been to the place of the battle.[11]

During the battle, when a tropical thunderstorm unleashed its fury and heavy rain pelted down over the Nui Dat base, the steam from overheated cannons, and cordite gas and smoke emanating from the artillery rounds being fired were hanging heavily around the gun lines. The smoke was so thick that several men had to be treated for smoke inhalation, as John explained:

I was trying to look after the fellows that were being overcome by the smoke and helping out a bit. And we'd also been mortared. A lot of the mortar and recoilless rifle rounds that came in on the night of the 17th [August] came into our area. And we took about five or six casualties.[12]

John appreciated being able to 'walk the ground' at Long Tan: 'To actually stand—I walked off a little while and looked down the road where that whole section was found dead the next morning. And, yeah, it was good going back.'[13]

However, veteran Ben Morris had a different reaction when he returned to Long Tan. 'I just find the place depressing in the fact that so many young people lost their lives on both sides.' Ben agreed that Long Tan is a commemorative site, adding, 'It represents the enemy and our blokes.'[14]

Fred Pfitzner was in South Viet Nam when the battle raged, and he reflected on what returning to the battle site meant for him:

You couldn't have been involved in that without being in some way affected by it. We were almost spot on—when we visited there—for the time when the action happened, and it had been raining. I mean, it was much better than going there in the middle of the dry and kicking up dust. So we were probably lucky to see Long Tan under those conditions. But you still don't get the sense of just how close to the Task Force base it was and what a potential bloody catastrophe the whole thing could have been. If we'd failed there, it could have completely changed the Australian national attitude to the war to the degree that the government probably would have had to do something about it. If we'd gone in there and lost some five or six hundred blokes, it would have been serious stuff. And that was a possibility had it not been [for] a great series of fortuitous events. Apart from the poor buggers who got knocked in it.[15]

Fred agreed the battle site had commemorative significance, adding:

Long after Nui Dat is developed and you're not allowed in there because there are people's houses and things, hopefully that Long Tan patch will remain. And you can't ask for better than that.[16]

A concert on the evening of 18 August starring entertainers Little Pattie and Col Joye was abandoned when the battle had been seriously joined. Little Pattie was whisked away by chopper back to Vung Tau, but Col Joye was not. Ron Shambrook revealed where Col Joye had gone:

I popped down there [to the concert] for about ten minutes and got some photographs of Little Pattie up on stage, and then I found out later that evening that they were still looking for Col Joye. Col hadn't gone back to Vung Tau and they didn't quite know where he was. The next morning I found out that Col Joye had spent the night in my company, Admin Company 5 RAR, boozing with some of my fellows and I thought, 'Well that is the end of a nice career Ron, you're gone now.' But it wasn't [laughs].[17]

Ron also believes Long Tan is an important commemorative site: 'I think it's very significant that the Cross is there and that it is maintained. It was a significant battle.'[18]

Peter Rogers served in South Viet Nam two years after the Long Tan battle, but still saw his visit to the site as being significant.

> I think I now realise how much it means to all of the veterans. We had a small service there. But I thought it was a bit superficial because we had to pick up the plaque before we went and then hang it on the Cross.[19]

The bronze plaque that Peter is referring to would normally be attached to the centre of the Cross, but as explained previously, it is held for safekeeping at the local police station in the village of Long Tan. It has to be collected—along with a policeman—before entering the site. Previous plaques have been souvenired and the Vietnamese officials are determined it will not happen again.

The Cross is a very simple, cast-concrete replica of the one that was erected on the third anniversary of the battle in 1969. The original Cross sits in a museum in Bien Hoa City. When asked if it mattered not having the names of the Australian fallen on the Cross, Ron Shambrook replied:

> I have been to—in many parts of the world—Anzac Day ceremonies and cemeteries. You don't remember the

few names that are on the cenotaph; you remember so
many, many more. And that [Long Tan] Cross for me did
exactly the same thing. It remembered. Had their names
been there, it may have been fine. But, you know, we still
remember anyway.[20]

Roger Wainwright saw his return to Long Tan as including
'paying your respects'. He had patrolled through the area
before and after the battle during 5 RAR's first tour of duty.
He concurs with many of his comrades on the significance
of the site:

It is the only Australian memorial in Viet Nam, and I
think from that perspective it has become a focal point. It
is very special. But to me on this particular trip there are
a couple of things—visiting my platoon position in Nui
Dat, and probably An Nhut—I'd put ahead of that on this
particular trip. But Long Tan's always special because of
that reason—having been the duty officer for a three-day
period when we were mortared during the actual battle,
and working in the 5 RAR command post . . . But being
back in that position again is quite moving.[21]

Tony White expressed similar sentiments on the emotional
tug of the Long Tan battlefield site.

I think if we're going to have any one thing to summarise
the Aussie involvement [in the war], then Long Tan is a
reasonable one within the province. It is very tasteful and
it's in the right location, and if we can keep the locals
on side so they don't bulldoze it, then that's going to be

wonderful. Because I'm sure for Aussies, it'll be like a sort of mini-Kokoda or Gallipoli.[22]

Peter Isaacs was more circumspect:

I think that it's just a Cross to those who died at Long Tan. I think it would not be appropriate to put up a memorial anywhere else to Australian and indeed New Zealand soldiers who died here. I think that it is appropriate, but I don't see it as any sort of centrepiece to Australia's sacrifice here. There were other battles—not quite the same significance as Long Tan like Coral and Balmoral which were much more bitter fights. So, no, to me it just represents Delta Company 6 RAR, and indeed the APC troop.[23]

Another version of events

Since the Cross was first erected in 1969, the former enemy have recognised its importance to Australian veterans who visit the site. When I first returned there in 1993, there was a small fence erected around the Cross and cement pillars holding plastic link-chain around the site, presumably to keep wandering cattle out. On the front right-hand pillar was a tablet inscribed in Vietnamese that roughly stated, inter alia: 'This was the site of a famous National Liberation Front victory wherein scores of Imperialist puppets were killed, several dozen armoured cars and tanks destroyed and several jet aircraft shot down.'

Unfortunately I did not note down the exact wording, probably because I was so incensed.

On a return trip in 1994, where I was distributing 500 kilograms of donated school supplies in the Long Dien District, I asked the chairman of the People's District Committee if he would consider removing the tablet as I thought it insulted the memory of all those soldiers who fought. As a former Viet Cong soldier, his mood instantly darkened; he was obviously not happy with my suggestion and nothing further eventuated. On the eve of a following visit in August 1996, in the presence of former Deputy Prime Minister Tim Fischer (himself a Viet Nam veteran, wounded in the Battle of Coral) I told Mr Fischer about the tablet. To my delight and surprise, the offending tablet was gone. It has never been replaced to my knowledge and was not there in subsequent visits I made in 2002 and 2005.

However, while the tablet has been physically removed from sight, the underlying view of history has not changed in the eyes of the government of the Socialist Republic of Viet Nam, which is responsible for all tourist activities and publications. In late 2006 Garry Adams came across the current edition of the *Ba Ria–Vung Tau Guidebook*, which gives the official version of the battle of Long Tan and the significance of the Cross (referred to as a 'stele', which is defined in *The Macquarie Dictionary* as 'an upright slab or pillar of stone bearing an inscription, sculptural design, or the like'). The entry in the guidebook reads:

The stele is a hard mix of concrete and steel. Although it is quite simple, it carries with itself a meaningful sense.

It was built by Australian Royal Force on August 18, 1969 in memory of fallen Australian soldiers on Southeast battlefields, particularly in a strike led by Australia and New Zealand on August 18, 1966. With an intention of occupying Ba Ria–Long Khanh, they were completely destroyed. The fallen left a great trace of sorrow for their wives and mothers, and countries. There have been thousands of Australian veterans who came back, wrote many articles on this stele, not to mention the fact that a complete book on this particular cross stele was published. On November 16, 1988, the Ministry of Culture and information voted it a historical heritage, following the Decision No. 1288 VH/QD.[24]

It would seem that nothing has really changed, and probably won't for at least a generation—and even then there may be nobody with the courage to rewrite the 'official' history that has been accepted for 40 years.

Leave the esky at home

The boorish conduct of some Australian men—presumably veterans—in the past at the battle site has threatened to have this sensitive location placed off limits to visiting Australians. Thankfully several groups have been able to convince the local authorities that the ill-mannered and stupid behaviour of a few is not typical of those who wish to pay their respects.

Bill Kromwyk was serving in the Anti-Tank (Tracker) Platoon of 6 RAR on their second tour when the Long Tan

Cross was erected. His platoon provided some of the local protection and picketed the ground when the Cross-raising ceremony took place. He remarked:

> I have heard a few bad reports about people going back with eskies full of beer and all that sort of stuff. And going in without permission and getting a lot of people offside. I have heard about these blokes and I think how stupid are you? I don't know what they are thinking; maybe they are not thinking.[25]

Tour guide Garry Adams confirmed the stories of how several years ago a group took beer in an esky to the site 'so the boys could share a drink' and behaved abominably.

The Vietnamese people have classified Long Tan as a sensitive site—and it has to be remembered that it is also the site where hundreds of soldiers from *275 Viet Cong Main Force Regiment* and *D 445 Battalion* also lost their lives.

There is now a large ceramic urn inside the Long Tan Cross site, and it is seen by the hosts as a sign of respect to place joss sticks in the urn, commemorating *all* who gave their lives on 18 August 1966.

As the former company commander of Delta Company 6 RAR, Major Harry Smith, MC, wrote in *Wartime* magazine, the official magazine of the Australian War Memorial:

> Although nowhere near the same scale, Long Tan will be remembered alongside Kapyong, Tobruk, and Gallipoli. I am saddened by the loss of life, and the tragic loss to all the loved ones, on both sides ... But we saved the Task Force base from what would have been a disastrous attack

by the 5000-strong *Viet Cong 5th Division*, and their influence in the province was reduced thereafter. That is why Long Tan has become so significant and is feted as the icon of the war for all Viet Nam veterans to commemorate those lost or maimed between 1965 and 1972.[26]

Part III

MAKING PEACE WITH THE PAST

Chapter 7

THE GAMUT OF EMOTIONS

The emotional impact of returning to a war zone will affect everyone differently. Education levels, ethnicity, religious beliefs, family upbringing and personal environment all shape the way we think and therefore how we react. We cannot throw a blanket over the group of individuals we call war veterans and expect them all to act the same way simply because they all served in the same war. Even men from the same rifle section or gun crew can experience different reactions on seeing their former tent lines, chopper pad and battle sites.

Tour guide Garry Adams is almost considered a 'local' as he spends most of the year working in Viet Nam. He was asked how he felt after his first trip back and he replied:

> I wasn't satisfied at all. I hadn't seen what I wanted to see. In the view of getting it out of my system, it never happened that way. It took me not quite twelve months to come back again for the second trip.[1]

Without doubt memories will be stirred and if the veteran is accompanied by mates with whom he served, the odd phrase or saying will crank up the brain cells and soon a wave of images will come flashing back. Not everyone will experience that feeling; some will be totally blank and offer

'I don't remember that' when everyone else will say, 'sure you do'.

But we are also talking about a war that happened more than three decades ago. A lot of water has passed under the bridge since then, and memories do fade. I recently saw a photograph of myself in Nui Dat, and simply cannot remember when and why the photograph was taken or who took it. Such is the impact of age upon the memory banks, as Ron Shambrook discovered when he returned to Long Son Island with the 5 RAR group, and couldn't reconcile the adjutant's recollection of the operational fly-in with his own version of events. They were able to clarify the situation with the help of a map, which showed that there had been two landing zones, which accounted for the conflicting memories. As Ron mused:

> Some of our memories aren't as good as we thought they were. And between your collective memories, it helps a lot. And I'm so delighted that I'm going back with a much broader and much clearer understanding of things ... I wouldn't have enjoyed it near as much if I were doing it by myself.[2]

Garry Adams has seen hundreds of veterans return to Viet Nam and offered these comments about the reactions he has observed:

> I think perhaps a few get rid of the ghosts that they may be harbouring, but I think for most of them it more or less gives them an idea of what Viet Nam is like now rather than what they think it was 30 years ago. They can see the

Posing for a group photo in front of an Iroquois helicopter at the War Remnants Museum in Ho Chi Minh City are, from left to right, Paul Greenhalgh, Peter Isaacs, Ted Heffernan, Roger Wainwright (rear), John Taske, Ron Shambrook (front), Tony White, Ben Morris and Fred Pfitzner. *Photo courtesy Ron Shambrook*

Standing in front of a B-52 bomb crater at the Fire Support Base Coral battle site, visiting veterans and partners listen to tour guide Garry Adams (third from left, pointing) describe the battle. *Photo courtesy Paul Greenhalgh*

At the risk of scaring the locals the 5 RAR pilgrimage group pose at Vung Tau in 2005, recreating a photograph taken of their group in 1966. Pictured are, from left to right: Dr Ted Heffernan, Dr Tony White, Ben Morris, Dr John Taske, Ron Shambrook, Roger Wainwright, Paul Greenhalgh, Peter Isaacs and Fred Pfitzner. *Photo courtesy Paul Greenhalgh*

The officers of 5 RAR's first tour of duty pose for a Mess photograph in 1966 before leaving on Operation Hardihood to secure the Australian Task Force base at Nui Dat. *Back row, left to right:* 2Lt Jack Carruthers, Lt Roger Wainwright, 2Lt John Deane-Butcher, 2Lt Dennis Rainer, Lt Greg Negus, Capt Ron Boxall, Capt Ron Bade, Capt Bob O'Neill, Capt Brian Ledan, 2Lt Bob Gunning, 2Lt Trevor Sheehan, Lt John Hartley, Lt Ralph Thompson, 2Lt John McAloney. *Centre row, left to right:* 2Lt Harry Neesham, Lt David Rowe, Mr John Bentley (Salvation Army), 2Lt Ted Pott, 2Lt Mick Deak, 2Lt Finnie Roe, Lt Bob Supple, 2Lt John Cook, Capt Don Willcox, Capt Bob Milligan, 2Lt Terry O'Hanlon, 2Lt John Nelson. *Front row, left to right:* Chaplain Ed Bennett, Capt Ron Shambrook, Maj Bert Cassidy, Maj Bruce McQualter, Maj John Miller, Maj Stan Maizey, LtCol John Warr, Maj Max Carroll, Capt Peter Isaacs, Maj Noel Granter, Maj Paul Greenhalgh, Capt Tony White, Chaplain John Williams. *Photo courtesy John Cook*

The hydrofoil ferry service docking at Vung Tau has become a very popular way to travel to the seaside resort town. The hills of Vung Tau are visible in the background. Veterans will be hard pressed to locate any former R&C haunts, but the town still has the charm it held 40 years ago. *Photo courtesy Ron Shambrook*

The harbour and hills of Vung Tau peninsula welcome visitors to the seaside resort much as they did the many Australian soldiers and sailors who came to the harbour aboard the HMAS *Sydney* during the war. *Photo courtesy Roger Wainwright*

The 5 RAR pilgrimage group pose in front of the Nui Thi Vais (also known as the 'Warbies' or 'Warburton Mountains') on their tour around the old Phuoc Tuy Province. From left to right are Dr Tony White, Roger Wainwright, Peter Isaacs, Ben Morris, Fred Pfitzner, Ron Shambrook and Paul Greenhalgh. *Photo courtesy Gary McKay*

The Nui Dat Medical Association, who had their first and last meeting in early 1967 prior to returning to Australia, celebrate and reminisce 38 years later very close to where they first downed some French pink champagne. Toasting the fact that they are still alive and upright are doctors John Taske, Tony White and Ted Heffernan. *Photo courtesy Tony White*

Paul Greenhalgh peers through the soft gloom of the rubber in Nui Dat near where 5 RAR established their original home in the Task Force base. Many veterans can place where their tent lines were during their stay in the area.
Photo courtesy Paul Greenhalgh

A veteran walks back from his old tent lines in the northern sector of the former Task Force base at Nui Dat. The rubber is once again being worked and a factory now stands close to where the aircraft refuelling point was located.
Photo courtesy Tony White

This road on the eastern flank of the Nui Dat base was once called Infantry Circuit and the three infantry battalions shared the avenue. Further south and beyond the photograph the road enters a prohibited zone where the current *D445 Battalion* is located. *Photo courtesy Garry Adams*

Standing amidst the ruins of what was the artillery command post at Nui Dat the 5 RAR tour group consult maps and memories as they survey the former Task Force base area. *Photo courtesy Peter Isaacs*

One of the few remaining signs of Australian occupation at Nui Dat is the ruins of the back gates to the Task Force base. *Photo courtesy Garry Adams*

Today, the local people ride their bikes through the Nui Dat rubber near the ruined gates. *Photo courtesy Peter Isaacs*

The 5 RAR pilgrims reflect on the battle at Long Tan in 2005 after a brief but moving informal remembrance service by several veterans who served in the battle area in 1966. *Photo courtesy Rupert White*

The Memorial Cross at Long Tan stands silent and sombre under the rubber canopy. The site has become iconic to veterans returning to Viet Nam and is one of only two foreign war memorials in the country. *Photo courtesy Elizabeth Stewart*

Embracing in front of the remains of The Horseshoe that had briefly carried the name Fort Wendy are Wendy Greenhalgh and her husband Paul, whose sub-unit was the first rifle company to occupy and begin fortification of the permanent fire support base in early 1967. Today the feature is being quarried for road base and is slowly disappearing. *Photo courtesy Tony White*

The view looking south-east from The Horseshoe with the edge of the Long Hais barely visible through an approaching afternoon thunderstorm. *Photo courtesy Garry Adams*

5 RAR Association President Roger Wainwright leaves a simple yet moving tribute to the officers and men of his rifle company who were killed in a mine incident outside the village of An Nhut on 22 February 1967.

Photo courtesy Roger Wainwright

Villagers tend to their rice crops east of Ba Ria and close to the village of An Nhut, with the Long Hai Hills in the background. *Photo courtesy Paul Greenhalgh*

Comparing notes and war stories in the Long Hais are former D 445 Battalion officer Lieutenant Hoang Ngan, 5 RAR platoon commander Roger Wainwright and RMO Dr Tony White. Mr Hoang runs the Long Hai museum and a small café in the Long Hai Hills. *Photo courtesy Rupert White*

Shrapnel scars and bomb-fractured rocks adorn the entrance to a former Viet Cong hospital set amongst the caves and enormous granite boulders in the Long Hais. The area has been allegedly cleared of mines but visitors should exercise caution when moving off defined paths and tracks. *Photo courtesy Garry Adams*

Above: Looking south towards the Long Hai Hills and the former Minh Dam Secret Zone, which had a reputation as a place you really didn't want to go if you were an infantryman. The Hills have once again recovered the growth that had been severely defoliated by chemical spraying. *Photo courtesy Garry Adams*

Facing page: Dr Ted Heffernan in front of a monastery where he once conducted a medical aid program during Operation Hayman on Long Son Island in early November 1966. The area had not changed much in the intervening years and it brought great delight to the doctor to see where he had once worked with the local Vietnamese community. *Photo courtesy Rupert White*

The ubiquitous hawkers and peddlers will pursue tourists almost anywhere to sell their souvenirs and goods. Ambushed and with nowhere to go atop the monument to the Viet Cong in Vung Tau are, in the foreground and from left to right, Rupert White, Dr Tony White and Doffy White. In the background, considering the merits of yet another T-shirt they don't need, are Fred Pfitzner and tour guide Garry Adams. *Photo courtesy Paul Greenhalgh*

Resplendent in their 5 RAR cravats and ready for a night out in Vung Tau are, from left to right, Ron Shambrook, Dr Tony White and Peter Isaacs. *Photo courtesy Tony White*

The ever busy Hoa Long markets are still a thriving meeting place for the local villagers who rely on fresh produce daily. The village was known to be pro-Viet Cong during the American War and supportive of anti-government activities.
Photo courtesy Roger Wainwright

Peter ('the Pirate') Isaacs entertaining a horde of Catholic school children in the town of Binh Gia where the 5 RAR pilgrims stopped for a rest. The friendliness of the local populace is one aspect that never fails to impress visiting veterans.
Photo courtesy Ron Shambrook

The opportunity to dine out in one of the many fine restaurants in Viet Nam was not passed up by the 5 RAR pilgrimage group when they had a sightseeing day and enjoyed lunch at the Ha Hoi Restaurant in Hanoi. *Photo courtesy Roger Wainwright*

The 5 RAR pilgrimage group pose on the steps of their hotel in Hanoi towards the end of their tour. Pictured standing from left to right are Dr Ted Heffernan, historian Elizabeth Stewart, tour guide Garry Adams, Roger Wainwright, Fred Pfitzner, Peter Isaacs (eye patch), John Taske, Tina Wainwright, Paul Greenhalgh (front), Ben Morris (beard), Joy Heffernan and Ron Shambrook. Seated are author Gary McKay and Wendy Greenhalgh. *Photo courtesy Paul Greenhalgh*

Vietnamese are real people; they have lives. They can be quite generous and friendly and it should give them a different perspective on what Viet Nam is like, but in peacetime rather than in war. I think all this business about 'lifting all the ghosts' and this sort of thing, maybe in some cases it works, but in a lot of other cases I think whatever memories they had about Viet Nam in wartime are still going to be there. But at least they can go back and look at it in a new perspective, and say, 'Well look at the country now', and maybe it is time to move on.[3]

Some men react in a fashion that others might find upsetting. I have seen men break down and cry, in some cases almost inconsolably. And on a personal level I've been 'hit between the eyes' when suddenly and unexpectedly a vivid memory came flashing back, and literally stopped me in my tracks. I needed to just sit down and think about what I had experienced and collect my thoughts before moving along. But these feelings will pass and it is one reason why returning with someone who understands what you have experienced in war is a good thing. Total strangers will not have a clue as to what you are feeling or why you are looking at a dry paddy field and sobbing.

Garry Adams recalled a few instances where this type of reaction occurred:

I have had a few occasions, particularly with the 'bush soldiers' . . . mostly the infantry and the field soldiers; you get to places and some of them do have problems. A place I have found that stirs up more memories than anywhere else is Cu Chi and the tunnels in Cu Chi. But especially at

Cu Chi when they walk into that narrow track and they are back in the bush again for the first time, and I have had guys that have stopped dead and can't take another step. I then have to take them by the arm and say, 'It's okay.' I was quite moved when you hear that drivel [Viet Cong propaganda] on that film [shown at the site] and I am more content to just walk away and sit down for a bit, and for some of them it never goes away. It doesn't, no matter what you have done in the meantime; whatever happened on those tracks always stays with you when you get back into that situation. It always comes back.[4]

Of all the places I have visited, Cu Chi is one that will bring back memories more than any other. The smell of the jungle, the proximity of the bush, the footpads and the dress of the soldiers that work in the military reservation all combine to evoke often powerful memories. The incident Adams was referring to at Cu Chi occurred on a visit in 2002 and involved former 6 RAR rifleman Steve Campling, who was suddenly overcome with emotion when he entered the jungle at the now very popular tourist destination. Steve needed to sit and relax and understand that what he experienced was common for a veteran; he was soon his normal self again. It was a reminder to all in the touring party just how much we can keep a lid on certain things and how easily it can be prised open. As Steve said of his visit to Viet Nam in 2002:

The only downside was the visit to the Cu Chi tunnels and my first encounter with the real 'J' [jungle] as I remembered it. It was raining; locals were walking along tracks through the undergrowth, and the sound of AK-47s being fired on the rifle range all combined to bring me 'undone'. I was overwhelmed . . . It took a good hour to regain my composure, along with the help of a couple of my travelling companions who were on their third or fourth trip back.[5]

The tunnels at Cu Chi are almost as they were during the war, but veterans who haven't been there should be warned that halfway through the complex there is a small theatrette that shows a propaganda film that is really quite offensive to anyone who fought against the Viet Cong. It is defamatory to Allied soldiers and also insults the intelligence of those who view the film. However, there is little point getting upset about it. As I said to my 21-year-old daughter Kelly after she watched the film in 2002 and asked me, 'Surely that's not right, Dad?', 'Winners are grinners and can rewrite their own history.'

Cathartic or not?

Some people believe returning to the war zone will have a cathartic effect and cleanse the suffering of the past. However, the term 'catharsis' is popularly misunderstood. As *The Macquarie Dictionary* notes, in psychological terms catharsis implies 'an effective discharge with symptomatic relief but not necessarily a cure of the underlying pathology'. In other words, just going back to Viet Nam will not necessarily resolve any underlying mental issues one might have with having served in the war zone. Dr Ted

Heffernan was asked if going back had been cathartic for him and he replied:

> Ah, no. To be honest I don't think so because I don't know that I have too many hang-ups about it all—I think because our role [as doctors] was a bit different. I wasn't coming out of there having killed people; I was really trying to help everyone. So that was pretty easy to do and in line with what I'd done before the first time I saw dead Diggers here. I'd seen dead people occasionally in car accidents and although it's terrible because they're young, it's not as much of an effect as it was on their fellow soldiers that were all looking and saying, 'There was a mate ... from this morning.' But it was sad and the only time I really reflected on the total wastage of young life was when I had to go down to Vung Tau and identify Peter Williams's body after the mine incident at An Nhut.[6]

You don't actually have to kill someone to be affected by the horrors of war. Ted was asked to go to the morgue and identify the bodies of the Australian soldiers killed, and the American sergeant in charge of the morgue (this was before the Australian morgue had been established in the field hospital at Vung Tau) began unzipping several body bags to find the Diggers. Seeing the rows of dead in the morgue, Ted thought, 'Well, jeepers. Look at this room full of plastic bags that were all fit young men three days ago.' When Ted returned to the site of the mine incident at An Nhut in 2005 it all came back. 'I thought about it again,' he said. 'I've often thought about that as the futility of war really, to be honest.'[7]

Ron Shambrook also didn't think there was too much catharsis in the trip; for him, it was more a case of 'the camaraderie with my colleagues. Reminiscing.' However, he added: 'It's brought back a lot of memories, mostly good. You can't turn back the past. If somebody's dead or wounded, that's occurred. You can't turn that back.'[8]

Ben Morris did find that his three trips back have been cathartic, and have gradually helped him to deal with post traumatic stress disorder (PTSD):

> Being back on the ground I have been able to scope it back down. It's a bit like peeling an onion. So this has been part of the onion-peeling process and I've been in this for fifteen years.[9]

Ben did, however, have some guidance for other veterans with PTSD who are thinking about returning:

> My advice would be first go to the Vietnam Veterans Counselling Service and talk some of your issues about Viet Nam through first. Because if you don't start to look at those, they're going to come out and grab you.[10]

Other veterans also expressed caution about expectations of catharsis. Peter Isaacs, whose main reason for undertaking the pilgrimage was 'to remember those young men', said he would recommend it for other veterans, 'But only on the basis of nostalgia and pilgrimage. Not to overcome any nightmares they might have.'[11]

The medicos in the group offered a similar view. John Taske advises veterans, 'It can be cathartic for them, but some people it may affect differently—they may just open old wounds.'[12]

Tony White agrees that 'veterans have a huge range of different ways of responding to the experience'. As a doctor, he notes:

> For some it's been a crushing thing. And some, I think, make the mistake of actually dwelling on the past and wallowing in it. I think that in a way is bad for them. But my feeling is that you don't live in the past, but you should be able to *visit* it. And this is what in fact we're doing. We're visiting the past and it's clarifying it in my mind, it's clarifying it for Doffy and Rupert. And so it's very good. For me it has always been the most important single year of my life. And, you know, most intense and vivid and so on. And so I wasn't expecting it to be any more or less than that. And that's how it turned out. It's been spot on.[13]

When Paul Greenhalgh was asked if he found the trip cathartic he initially said no. Then his wife Wendy chimed in, pointing out gently: 'Yes, but you had a change of heart—you didn't want to come. So I think that in itself is cathartic. That you decided you would come.' Paul looked at his wife and replied, 'Alright. Yes babe.' And she looked lovingly at her husband and rejoined with, 'And you're smiling about it.'[14]

Grieving

When servicemen were killed in Viet Nam their bodies were flown back to Australia, normally on a C-130 Hercules RAAF transport aircraft. At first, the dead were to be buried locally, but following protests by serving soldiers Kranji Military Cemetery in Singapore was chosen as the burial place. Then those who died in Viet Nam were buried in the Australian section of the British War Cemetery at Terendak in Western Malaysia. This policy was later also overturned, and remains were repatriated to Australia for burial or disposal at the next-of-kin's request.[15]

If a serviceman was killed during an operation his body would be choppered or driven out of the battle site, then repatriated back to Australia. His mates would continue patrolling and fighting and maybe not return to camp for weeks after the event. A memorial service might have been held for those killed when the unit was back in Nui Dat or Vung Tau, but the pace of operations often meant that this service might not be attended by those wanting to grieve or to say goodbye. Consequently, there was often very little closure to the loss.

Returning to Viet Nam will often reignite that need for grieving, and it will not be uncommon to have those emotions impact upon the veteran when those memories are stirred up again. It is part of the process and should be allowed to run its course. Laying of wreaths is a delicate issue in Viet Nam today, and veterans are urged to instead place a single flower at a place for remembrance to avoid upsetting local feelings.

Don't rush it

The returning veteran should avoid being pushed and hurried through the experience. Avoid the 'Day 5, this must be Da Nang' syndrome, and make sure that there is time to see everything that you want to, and have enough time in the itinerary to simply stop, look and listen. As Ben explained:

> I had a bit of trepidation in the fact that I'd seen some earlier tours go through Vung Tau when I was there and I felt sorry for the people because they were rushed into Vung Tau and rushed out. They really didn't have a chance to see anything. I think the design of this tour—having three days to be able to go over the ground reasonably slowly—is what was needed. There is this need to be able to stop, reflect and to relive.[16]

Ben explained, 'The memories are vivid every day. Going back over the ground in some ways, it gave me a chance to demystify some of it and put it in perspective.' As his group walked around Nui Dat, Ben found value in 'sitting at 5 RAR headquarters, and then standing on top of the hill . . . and just being able to stop, reflect and just enjoying it'.[17]

Tina Wainwright believed Roger had felt the impact of returning to his old lines and conducting a small memorial service at Tiger Pad in the rubber plantation. Such events can take time to digest. When being interviewed, she looked at her husband and said:

> . . . that night you were pretty emotional if you remember, because you felt like you would have liked to have spent more time. But I remember you said to me, 'That was my home for a year.' You know. 'It's like that was where we pushed off from.'[18]

Time to look, reflect and ponder is important on a pilgrimage; after all it is why you are there. Roger understood
that there were limitations to time and space on the tour,
but simply added: 'I would have liked no more than half an
hour just to wander round and reflect. [Look at] not just
my positions but some of the other platoon positions as
well and where the company kitchen was.'[19]

Also, it takes time to retrace old steps—but carrying old
maps and records can help. Roger claims he has a good
memory (he still owes me $10 from a bet in 1985), but said
he did some homework before returning with the 5 RAR
pilgrims:

> I think I've got a pretty vivid memory of everything that
> happened over that period of time. And I did refresh
> myself by perusing Bob O'Neill's book *Vietnam Task*
> again. And I had a marked map with me that I carried
> in 1966 ... I showed it to Tina when we stopped on
> Route 15, and I could identify the exact spot where I
> was wounded and nine people in my platoon were also
> wounded. And down on Long Son Island, Gary [McKay]
> and I went round and I had the grid reference of LZ
> Dagwood where we landed, and Gary actually identified it
> from a distance through his binoculars. And I said, 'Yep.
> There it is. There's that spur where the helicopter
> landed.'[20]

Tony White has had the advantage of having his old 8-mm
home movie film to revisit over the years, so he had a pretty
good idea of what it all looked like back in 1965. But
touring around in an air-conditioned bus 40 years later

brought an entirely new perspective to an old experience, as he explained:

> If you could subtract all that horrible ribbon develop-
> ment, which is obviously a plague upon the face of the
> province, it's very much the same. But I tell you, when you
> were with the unit, distances were a lot greater. I mean,
> here we are whistling around and going up to Xuyen Moc
> in an hour. That was the sort of thing that you'd think, oh,
> that's a big chopper ride. So the distances then appeared
> to be big, much bigger than they really are. I mean, we had
> just this tiny area when you think of it, and that run up to
> Binh Ba, which was quite a safari back then. It was a dirt
> track. So it was that sort of elasticity of distance which was
> the most noticeable thing to me.[21]

Letting bygones be bygones

Staff Sergeant Bob Hann returned to Viet Nam in 1993 on an organised tour with mates from Delta Company, 4 RAR. Bob was in a pilgrimage group that was invited to socialise with former members of the *D 445 Battalion* at Long Phuoc Hai, but he was a bit uncertain how he and his fellow grunts would be received. The reception was not quite what he expected:

> I came away with an immense respect for our former
> enemies. We were invited to share a meal and more than
> a few drinks with our former foes at what could best be
> described as a Viet Cong RSL. The hospitality shown to
> us by people so poor was incredible. Even now I pull out

the photographs and ponder on what was a remarkable day. It was even more remarkable when you consider that their English was at least as fluent as our Vietnamese.[22]

Bob found his own pilgrimage highly worthwhile:

> I recommend it to anyone prepared to listen. It is a beautiful country populated by hard working, cheerful people who could teach us a thing or two about making the best of what you have.[23]

Another veteran on that tour was Garry Heskett. I was also present, and we too were stunned by the total lack of animosity or angst from the ex-Viet Cong soldiers. It may sound like a cliché, but when the eighteen soldiers from Delta Company 4 RAR and the group of D 445 men came together and sank a few—*quite* a few!—beers, and then shared a meal, we were indeed 'brothers in arms'. The camaraderie was palpable. Stories were being told through interpreters, jokes were being shared and, in a few cases, bullet wounds were being shown. Garry said he came away from that meeting with:

> a feeling of self-achievement that I was able to locate and identify areas that for various reasons one way or another had an impact on me, which provided some closure. And finally—being able to share those experiences with former brothers in arms . . . I was impressed by the warmth of our reception from the majority of the people.[24]

Peter Isaacs came halfway around the world from the United Kingdom to join his 5 RAR mates and found that the expectations and reservations he had quietly harboured did indeed manifest themselves after he arrived in country. He was glad he participated in the pilgrimage:

> The apprehensions I had have turned out to be entirely predictable and true because I thought there would be considerable urban sprawl which has turned out to be the case, and I never like to see forest destroyed and ghastly advertisements put up all over the place. It happens all over the world and why should this be the exception? I was pleased that Nui Dat was pretty well as I remembered it when we got there. That remains as it was then, and I have to say it's been a moving experience.[25]

But this scarred, hardened infantryman with one leg and one eye and several campaigns under his belt articulated another emotion that can also be felt—especially on the first trip back:

> I've actually felt a little detached somehow. On the one hand, over the last 39 years since we were here, it's all seemed to be like yesterday on many occasions. Then one thinks about all the things that have happened in the middle and it seems a long time ago. Wandering round the places that we knew before, it has seemed a very long time ago. And it's a bit like going back to school in a way. After all, we were—many of us—not that long out of school. I mean, I was 25 or so but, you know, young and impressionable. And now I'm not young and impressionable. So I've been detached and actually not as moved as I thought I would have been.[26]

When the 5 RAR tour group visited the Long Hai Hills and were introduced to a former enemy officer, Peter was the only one in the group who avoided shaking the man's hand. When later asked why, Peter explained his reaction:

> I had no wish to shake him by the hand. My memory of the Viet Cong is they were a ruthless and murderous bunch. When I flew into the three villages that used to make up Binh Gia in 1966, I was told by one of the three Roman Catholic priests that had accompanied the inhabitants on their long journey from North Viet Nam after the 1953 Accords that the Viet Cong had abducted one of the [village] headmen, taken him across the paddy fields into the forest to the north and the next day, invited the villagers to come and see him. The Viet Cong had cut his legs off at the knees and put him in an ant heap as an 'example' of what non-cooperation could result in. And whilst he may have been an ordinary soldier, I don't know. And I didn't shake his hand; I didn't want to be rude, but, no. That is why I didn't want to meet any former VC in the Long Hai Hills or anywhere else.[27]

Those memories and perceptions are something that the pilgrim will have to confront. Yes, war is a brutal and horrific event, but this does not of course condone some of the cold-blooded atrocities perpetrated by the Viet Cong as a deliberate policy within their revolutionary warfare doctrine. Personally I've found it best to put the past behind me and move forward and accept the former foe as being similar to myself: 'just a soldier doing his job'.

Peter has reassessed how he looks upon his participation in the Second Indochina War.

> My reservations now are, after seeing the development
> that has taken place under a Communist regime, had we
> not come here it would probably have ended up like this
> anyway, because oil and gas would have been found and
> that is undoubtedly the life blood of the economy at the
> moment. I thought at the time we were right to come and
> fight. With the benefit of almost 40 years' hindsight, I
> think maybe we shouldn't have come here. It hasn't made
> any difference. But at the same time I don't regret it.[28]

Another thing that upset Peter is that the government
has apparently practically bulldozed into the ground many
ARVN graveyards and cemeteries. It seems incredible
that this would be done as a matter of policy, but it appears
to be the case. As Peter noted: 'I would like to have met
some former ARVN soldiers, but they don't exist in today's
Viet Nam. There are splendid memorials to the Viet Cong,
but the graveyards of ARVN soldiers have been totally
obliterated.'[29]

Infantryman Bill Kromwyk has embraced the Vietnamese people in more ways than one, marrying a
Vietnamese lady he met on a pilgrimage there in 2001,
several years after he was divorced. The strongest emotion
he came away with on his first visit was:

> The hospitality of the people, I think, and no sign of ani-
> mosity. That really struck me. If you respect them they
> will be very hospitable and helpful to you, and okay watch

out, because they are going to try and fleece you for every dollar that you have got.[30]

Bill would urge veterans to 'show respect—that is a big one. I think a lot of Australians have not been doing that, just from reports that I have had from other people, and remember that you are in *their* country.'[31]

John Taske explained his own feelings after meeting a former Viet Cong soldier at Long Hai:

> I don't know how the rest of the fellows think, but soldiers are soldiers—you've got a lot more in common sometimes with the enemy than you have with other people you meet, because they've been through the same things as you.[32]

Similarly to Bill Kromwyk's experience, described in Chapter 1, the fact that the enemy were 'just blokes doing their jobs like us' was driven home when John looked at a wallet retrieved from a dead Viet Cong soldier not long after he arrived in country in 1966. He recalled thinking, 'God, poor bugger. He was just like us and now he's gone. Some family's missing him.'[33]

Ron Shambrook met Lieutenant Hoang Ngan at Long Hai and reflected on his encounter:

> That was fine. He had a job to do in war and I had a job to do in war. I don't have resentment against particular people. If I knew they were the ones who did the murdering and the torturing of civilians and people like that I would have a different view. But until I'm aware of that, he's a fellow human being just doing his job.[34]

To go or not to go?

After returning for the first time in 1993, I can honestly say that I found it a healing process that allowed me to mentally move on. I felt more at peace after going back, and every subsequent visit has been more enjoyable, despite several unsettling incidents and run-ins with the Vietnamese bureaucracy over bungled permits in 2002. After that visit I did have terrible nightmares for a fortnight or so, which resolved with the help of counselling. I returned again in 2005 and had no flashbacks, nightmares or anxiety. Everything was fine, and I can't wait to go back again.

Veterans who have made the journey back have been tremendously impressed by the genuine warmth and friendliness of the Vietnamese people. Without exception all will tell you that the decision to go back is a highly personal one.

Ian Ryan, a veteran from a former pilgrimage, put it rather colourfully:

> I would highly recommend going back to anyone. It is like putting the lid on a garbage tin properly. If you do not put it on fully and tightly, the smell of the rotting garbage just permeates your whole mind and soul. You can never get rid of the stench! [Going back] just puts closure on your life.[35]

He added: 'It was closure of a chapter in my life that had been conveniently tucked away in the back of my mind; [I was] hoping it would just go away with time. It never does.'[36]

Tour guide and leader Garry Adams believes going back with men from your own unit works well. After leading dozens of tour groups, he remarked: 'Groups like the 5 RAR pilgrimage officer group are excellent because they all know each other; they have been bonded for a long time, they have kept in contact and there are no hassles.'[37]

Being accompanied by partners is something to consider as well. Garry Adams has seen groups with and without and he believes it is up to the veteran and their partner to decide, but he made this observation:

Partners can be a big help in coming back to Viet Nam for some of the fellows, especially the ones who are a bit wobbly about things. Their partners generally tend to stabilise them. But then again you can get occasions, which I have seen, where the partners can be absolutely destructive. The boys want to go out and have a drink in a bar, or have a wander around with their mates and they are more or less shackled into their hotel rooms and not allowed to go. I have heard more than one or two decent old shouting matches in the corridors of hotels just purely because of that. So it can be double-edged, but I would say that 85 per cent of the partners who come back here are excellent, and then you get the other 15 per cent that should never have come. They should have just let them [their partners] come on their own. And if they come they should just shut up and let the fellers go to places like Long Tan and Nui Dat and enjoy themselves; just touch base there rather than [say], 'Aw, what are we doing here?

How long are we going to be here? Where are the toilets? What did we come to this place for?'[38]

Women will also need to accept rudimentary conditions and toilets, but Gail Campling, who accompanied her husband Steve on a pilgrimage in 2002, offered this insight on the benefits of travelling with partners:

> It was a wonderful experience for me as I appreciated more what our troops went through. I would recommend partners go as well, but I could understand some veterans would find it even more confronting with their partners present. They may not want their partners to see them distressed or disturbed. I am sure Steve appreciated me being there, mainly to hear and see first-hand some of what he experienced. I don't think he could possibly relate to me the emotions and experiences had I decided not to go. Going with the veteran provides love and support as well when they are confronted with their 'ghosts'; someone to lean on that isn't as affected (in the same way) as those around them [other vets].[39]

The mateship experienced on the 2005 trip by the 5 RAR group was a special element that all the men commented on. As Paul Greenhalgh remarked, 'What a wonderful group we had. I mean, it was just magic. I didn't really know what to expect from them all. But we had no show ponies, no loud people. It just worked smoothly.'[40]

Garry Adams points out that the 5 RAR group were also fortunate in that their area at Nui Dat is accessible, and this made for smooth sailing:

They have seen what they want to see and we are probably lucky in some ways that the 5 RAR area is easy to get into and probably easier than some of the others. We couldn't go back to 8 RAR's area in Nui Dat or 3 RAR's area because it is just off limits [D 445 Battalion military garrison]. And the areas that the first tour fought in or served in were all reasonably close in to the Task Force base and so in that sense it was easier for them to get around and have a look at things.[41]

However, it won't all be plain sailing. There will be times during a visit when the locals can get to you, especially the hawkers and beggars who push themselves upon Westerners. Regardless of season, weather or terrain they will hound, harass and follow the tourist to the ends of the earth. They will even follow your tourist bus from one site to another, waving their products at you as they drive along. The best strategy is to just grin and bear it and give a polite 'no thank you' (preferably in Vietnamese), and never enter into argument about price or other purchases you may have made—you will lose every time! Hawkers and beggars are right in your personal space from the moment you step out onto the footpath in any major town in Viet Nam, but it is part and parcel of touring in much of Asia. To stop and buy or simply haggle is akin to opening a jar of honey on a picnic; you will be hit with a swarm of T-shirt sellers, dodgy watch purveyors and the occasional pick-pocket. So buyer beware.

Veteran Derrill De Heer has returned to Viet Nam several times, and would enthusiastically urge other veterans to consider making the return visit. However, he would encourage them to read up on the country beforehand, and 'make an effort to understand the culture, religions, history. It's rich and it's great.'[42]

As a final word, he added:

> But before you do, decide what you are going back for. You will not find the past. The population of the country is 80 million. There have been 40 million born since the war ended, and their young are not interested in their history, so don't expect them to be interested in you. Go to enjoy, don't go and be sorry for the past, move on, make it a positive experience for yourself.[43]

The trick cyclist's (psychologist's) view

Robyn Nolan is married to Viet Nam veteran and author Peter Nolan,[44] whose brother also served in South Viet Nam with the SAS. Robyn holds a Masters degree in clinical psychology, and began working with veterans in 1981 when she was doing her internship at the Veterans' Administration Hospital in Washington, DC. At that time veterans were quite young, and research was only just beginning on the subject of PTSD. Robyn dealt with Australian Viet Nam veterans from 1989 until she retired in 2005, and as a guesstimate has seen and worked with several hundred veterans during that time.

I asked Robyn for her professional perspective on the possible reactions the veteran may experience on returning to Viet Nam, and she offered these observations.

Well, when anyone goes back to a place that was important to them at any time, they have all sorts of reactions, from very enjoyable reactions—nostalgia and remembering the good times—but as well as that, remembering the bad times perhaps, that they might have had there. So it will just trigger memories and it depends on each veteran and each veteran's experiences in Viet Nam as to how they will react to the situation.

A lot of veterans have reported to me that they have found it a very healing experience, although they became distressed. Most said that they *did* become distressed at some point during their visit. Some felt annoyed at the way that the current Vietnamese talk about the war: in terms of them winning the war and the Americans and Australians losing the war. Although the veterans say they understand that, but at times, if they had been involved in a battle where friends were lost, then they found that very difficult. But others felt compassion towards the Vietnamese and in fact I know that some have actually taken on projects in Viet Nam to assist the Vietnamese. Others say they are surprised that Viet Nam has recovered from the war; many are surprised that there is very little left of where they might have been and that they have actually had trouble finding those places. They have looked for places of which they had memories.

I think there has been a healing process for some in that they have [previously] avoided dealing with or thinking about Viet Nam. Others have dealt with it in a superficial way by mostly thinking about the good times, I guess, and trying not to think about anything that was difficult for them. To them, Viet Nam is as it was then, and when they return, actually confronting the reality of the situation as it is now, I think that changes them. And it also makes them recognise the reality of where they are now and how far they have journeyed.[45]

On a visit back to Viet Nam in 2002, I was arrested along with tour leader Garry Adams and 3 RAR (second tour) veteran Bob McDonnell, and incarcerated in a holding room in the police station just south of where the battles of Coral and Balmoral were fought. This was somewhat ironic, as Garry Adams was visiting the spot to assist the local People's District Committee to locate a mass grave at the Fire Support Base Coral battle site. It was an administrative mix-up in permits for sensitive sites, but the local police officer was adamant in holding us miscreants for an afternoon, and out of mobile telephone range of Ho Chi Minh City. Eventually, just before dusk, the problem was sorted out and we returned safely to Saigon. However, upon returning to Australia I suffered horrific nightmares for fourteen days and was concerned that one might become reality, so I sought medical help. After being referred to the Vietnam Veterans Counselling Service I was referred to a psychiatrist who diagnosed PTSD, and then referred to Robyn for counselling. Consequently I have come to realise what impact events can have on veterans and how they can be treated.

For the benefit of other veterans, I asked Robyn what type of counselling and preventive measures they could undertake to make their journey less traumatic. She replied:

Of course there are lots of veterans who had problems almost immediately after returning from Viet Nam, for reasons that we know about. The Viet Nam War being a war that wasn't accepted by a lot of Australians made it different. So there were those difficulties. But for a lot of those veterans who haven't let themselves think about what happened, [returning to Viet Nam has] probably brought back a lot of those memories and they have been in a situation where they can confront the memories, and as I said before, accept the reality of how long ago it was and how the [Vietnamese] people have recovered.[46]

Because we are all different in our psychological makeup, it therefore follows that we all have different reactions to various stressors in our lives. Robyn Nolan tackled this issue when asked to describe how we would expect to react:

We *are* different, but similar as well. People have lots of different experiences in Viet Nam to begin with. We know from the research that just being involved in any war is traumatic for everybody. Having to kill people: that is something that you had to be trained to do, because that is not something that we normally do, and [today] there is a lot of research that looks at those sorts of issues and tries to prepare people for those kinds of things. In the Viet Nam era, there was none of that, and people were sent to Viet Nam. Some people were highly trained people who had been in the military for quite some time and were expecting what they were going to run into.

Others, as you know, were called up and given a lesser amount of training and sent to Viet Nam.[47]

Many National Servicemen that I've spoken to weren't aware that they could have avoided going to South Viet Nam if they wanted to. But they believe the main reason they went was because their group—the group that they were called up with and trained with—were going, and they didn't *not* want to go with them; probably an extreme example of peer pressure in a macho environment. Robyn Nolan agreed, but added: 'Yes, but what tended to be more the experience that I confronted was that it was more a case of not wanting to be *excluded*.'[48]

Robyn outlined other reasons veterans can experience a whole range of reactions on returning to Viet Nam.

Everybody had a different role; I guess if you were in a battalion everybody had similar roles and different experiences. They came into the Army with different backgrounds, and we know that people whose backgrounds were very difficult for them—perhaps they had problem childhoods, and I certainly saw people who did have that—then they probably had less opportunity to get away from those sorts of situations. They wouldn't have had that support that other people might have had. Having said that though, we do know from the research that post traumatic stress disorder can strike anybody, and it doesn't matter who you are, basically. It has a lot to do with your experiences and how you were supported during and after the event. It is a very complicated matter and not everybody who went to Viet Nam has post traumatic stress disorder anyway.[49]

Robyn's observations hit the nail on the head, and also address what seems to be a public perception that because a veteran served in South Viet Nam, they are automatically—and as colourfully described by one American Army psychologist I met in California in 1987—'fucked in the haid'. The Appendix discusses PTSD in detail and is designed to give the veteran a brief and uncomplicated look at what the disorder is and how to deal with the problem.

Robyn expanded a little on PTSD:

Many veterans probably have elements of post traumatic experience, but not necessarily the full-blown disorder. Many don't even know that they have got the disorder. They just accept that they get the memories, flashbacks, nightmares, and problem times that they have had; that is just the way that it is and [they] haven't bothered to do anything about it. I have spoken to a couple of colleagues about this, and we do know that some people without any symptoms go off to Viet Nam and then return with quite bad clinical symptoms; [in these cases it can] look like they just got it [PTSD], but they didn't, they already *had* the problem but they were just not dealing with it very well.

Having said that, I don't know whether there is any research or if anyone has carried out any research on people returning from visiting a battleground, but my own experience has been that most of the veterans that I have seen have probably been in therapy anyway before

they went, so they are a bit better prepared and found it
a healing experience. So I guess it might have to do with
how well prepared you are and who you go with.[50]

On a personal note, I did feel the need to speak with a
clinical psychologist and answer some basic questions
about preparing to return to Viet Nam before I actually
went. I asked Robyn whether it was helpful for veterans, if
they did decide to go back, to return with their spouse or
partner. Her view was:

> It depends on the veteran. Some veterans are very group-
> oriented and have maintained contact with their former
> mates in the Service and I think enjoy going as a group
> that they served with in Viet Nam and they therefore
> had similar experiences in Viet Nam. So it makes sense
> for them to go back to Viet Nam and to different places
> where they had served, and they could have a joint
> memory of what happened, and support each other.
>
> Some have had their spouses with them and I think
> most of the spouses of Viet Nam veterans have been used
> to dealing with the veterans' problems for a long time—if
> they have got any—but they can certainly give them
> support. If they have been married for a very long time
> they are pretty supportive of each other, they are probably
> good friends—best friends—so I think it is not a bad
> thing to have your best friend with you to be supportive of
> you, but I think that if you went with a group of people
> who you knew, I think that would probably at least give
> you that support.[51]

But what of the veteran who wants to go on their own and 'do their own thing'? What would be the most likely scenario they could face with regard to psychological and emotional reactions?

> If they went on their own and they didn't have anyone there to reflect with them on their experiences and support them, then that could be difficult for them. I know from the readings of the American experiences, the men were quite surprised because they would suddenly have a problem experience when they weren't expecting it ... I remember reading about when some of them went back down into the tunnels, and one of the chaps who had really been quite impressed with the Vietnamese and the way things had been going along, and how well they had been received, took umbrage at the presentation [the Viet Cong propaganda film at Cu Chi] by the people there and got really angry and upset.[52]

As discussed previously, the film at Cu Chi is fairly confronting, and the only time I've seen a veteran distressed was (Steve Campling) in that theatrette. Robyn shared some American observations that 'there was no humility in the NVA victory; perhaps we don't deserve it'. The War Remnants Museum (previously known as the War Atrocities Museum) in Saigon was also mentioned in an after-tour report, in which she said one soldier was quoted as saying, 'But we certainly don't deserve the treatment from the museum either and we are angry.'[53]

Robyn added that it isn't always easy to tell if a veteran is having a reaction, or what sort of reaction they may be experiencing.

Often we see somebody on television, maybe an old
World War Two veteran, crying at a site. Okay, that is very
nice for all of us to sit and say, 'Well isn't that nice that
they had that experience', but it may have been healing
for that person, or it may not have been, we don't know.
You can't tell just from looking at somebody what they
are experiencing and you don't know what the after-
effects of that are going to be, and nor does the person
experiencing it until they leave—and perhaps later they
are troubled by things and don't know why they are
troubled by things.[54]

Returning to Viet Nam will most likely immediately
trigger memories in veterans, both good and bad.

The most common thing is to have the memories as
soon as you are there—as is the case wherever we go. If
I go back to wherever I went to school I will have some
memories; if I go back to where I did nursing training
or went to university, I have some memories. And the
memories are good or bad depending on your experiences. So they are going to have those memories and
they may even have flashbacks, which are vivid daytime
memories, and a lot of veterans have had those in
Australia. This is while on the scene; they may re-
experience the feelings they had while they were there,
so they may experience fear or anxiety.[55]

Veterans will also remember the good times, and have a
good laugh about lots of things they did ... and didn't
do. When they return home, some of those memories

may continue; psychologists describe this behaviour as 're-experiencing' things. As Robyn said:

> When you are confronted with any kind of trauma, you may experience symptoms such as anxiety, re-experiencing, flash-backs, problems sleeping, problems concentrating. Usually that eases over time—say several weeks—but it can continue. Veterans who have had very long experiences—they may have been doing a number of patrols, been involved in a number of battles, been in the areas with mortars landing—may continue to relive the horrors of some of those situations if they have been back to Viet Nam.[56]

However, Robyn points out that this can be therapeutic: 'we [the psychology profession] regard confronting the situation as better than not confronting it.' Perhaps the adage is true that 'You can run from tigers but cannot run from your fear.' Robyn explained:

> Avoidance is one of the symptoms [of PTSD], and so we prefer that people don't avoid. But they have to be prepared for that—they can't suddenly be plonked back into the situation. You have to talk to the person about it.[57]

When some soldiers returned from Viet Nam during and after the war they suffered severe nightmares. This appears to be a common reaction for those exposed to the horrors of war.

> Nightmares are very common. Our brains are always processing things so you will probably have a lot of nightmares, which may resemble a situation that you were in in the past—or may not. They may just be unpleasant. Some

people might then do some of those avoidance behaviours that they have probably practised all of their lives, where they might overuse alcohol or other substances to help them sleep because they might be having trouble sleeping.[58]

Personal relationships may suffer when veterans who are losing sleep or are anxious become grumpy and irritable (psychologists call this 'hyper-arousal'). If unpleasant symptoms persist, Robyn would encourage veterans who aren't already in therapy to go and talk to somebody, even if it is only their local GP, as there are very many helpful strategies to help relieve their distress. As mentioned, I experienced delayed-onset PTSD some 29 years after my service in South Viet Nam, as a result of being incarcerated very briefly on a return visit in 2002, but as I discovered, PTSD is a condition you can learn to manage yourself; however, this may not apply to everyone as psychological makeup varies from person to person. You may need to be medicated for a period of time, but then again you may not. The important thing is to seek help.[59]

If you feel you may be succumbing to the effects of PTSD, please seek medical advice at the earliest opportunity. The Vietnam Veterans Counselling Service is established Australia-wide and is able to assist veterans with psychiatric and psychological counselling, and, if required, medication. All veterans are entitled to free counselling whether they have a Gold Card or not.[60]

The seven Ps

Just like the old Army saying that 'Prior Preparation and Planning Prevents a Piss-Poor Performance', veterans wanting to return to Viet Nam should apply the seven Ps. Robyn recommends that veterans who have already been seeing a therapist, even if it was quite a while ago, may want to contact that person, tell them they are going to Viet Nam, and just review some of the coping strategies that they have already learned.

There are many self-help books and a lot of useful information on the Internet for those who'd like to read up on the subject, or if you would like to have a chat to someone, contact your local Vietnam Veterans Counselling Service.

'Stress inoculation training' is also an option, and is something that is quite commonly done. Psychologists help prepare people to face their fears by gradually exposing them to fearful situations and teaching them better coping strategies to help manage and reduce their reactions.

Some veterans may wish to be 'debriefed' when they get back home after their trip, but Robyn emphasises that this is very much an individual decision.

It depends on whether they feel the need. There are two types of treatment; we call these defusing and debriefing. Defusing is what you do on the spot, where it is real—like a car accident, where you stand there and chat away to the guy, this happened and that happened, etc. Debriefing is something you can do further down the track and it really is just allowing you to talk about the experiences—rather than avoid talking about them at all.[61]

Debriefing in and of itself won't necessarily prevent you having PTSD, but it does at least give you an opportunity to get some support. If you feel that things are going round and round in your head, then it's probably best to talk to somebody about it.

Chapter 8
REFLECTIONS

This chapter gathers together reflections of the veterans, their partners and children on the 5 RAR tour in 2005, for the benefit of other veterans who are contemplating returning to the battlefields of Viet Nam. There are very few negative comments from the veterans, and this is not because they have been edited out, but because there were very few negative aspects to report. Here the tour members offer their personal thoughts on what they came away with from their pilgrimage.

Almost all of the veterans I have interviewed and chatted with about their return to Viet Nam have emphasised the value they extracted from going back. Common responses included phrases such as 'I'm glad I did it' and 'it gave me closure'. I cannot recall anyone who regretted their return visit. Many veterans said it was just a great experience being there with their former brothers in arms and that the bond created in wartime was just as strong four decades later. Of those who returned to Viet Nam with their partner, most said it strengthened their relationship. Many wives agreed that going back gave them a greater appreciation of what their partner had experienced and, after seeing their loved one back in the former war zone, they feel closer and understand their partner's reactions and behaviour more than before.

The 5 RAR veterans

Paul Greenhalgh was 'extremely glad' that he made his pilgrimage with the 5 RAR group in 2005. Paul felt that his experiences and memories had been reinforced and validated, and that it had been a fulfilling experience for both him and his wife. Indeed, he added: 'It would have been quite shallow and hollow if Wendy hadn't been here with me.' He mused:

> Going to Nui Dat and going to The Horseshoe were the two biggest things for me . . . They have been very significant experiences for me. Forget the changes [in Viet Nam], it doesn't matter. Just to physically go back and see it . . . The memories are there. They're not all dark and 'dirgy' memories. They're very positive ones from a very positive year in my life.[1]

Paul also had 'a buzz' at seeing the natural gas and oil industry development in Ba Ria–Vung Tau Province. As he explained, 'My second career was in the natural gas industry. So I always had an interest in those flames [at the plant in Ba Ria] and to hear and see what happened to it.' He added, 'It's funny, you go back in life and you often find things are smaller when you go back. But I was quite surprised how big that hill was at Nui Dat, even though half of it had been chewed off the top.'

Paul, whose 5 RAR rifle company went with 6 RAR back into the battlefield on 19 August 1966, found going back to Long Tan somewhat 'spooky'. 'Those sorts of feelings can send fuzziness up your backside,' he said. Paul believes

the Memorial Cross at Long Tan is very special, and recog-
nises its iconic value to Australians. 'But we have got to
realise it's their country,' he added. 'And all this confusion
about who won and who lost—saving face. Well, that's the
reality of life. Thank God we've got something.'

When asked about the small memorial service that his
group observed at Tiger Pad, Paul explained it was:

> in memory of four of our company that died. We only lost
> four which was pretty lucky . . . It pulled things together.
> And also in memory of the second tour of 5 RAR. I'm so
> glad that we mixed the two together rather than just do
> our own memories and own names.[2]

Dr Ted Heffernan was also 'very glad' that he returned
to Viet Nam. It allowed him 'to see the enormous change
in the country. To see how well the country's done since
we left. It's incredible. It's a bloody hive of industry. It's
fantastic.' And like many others, he found the Vietnamese
'terrific people'.

Returning with his wife Joy was important to Ted:

> I think it's a good thing really to point out to her where
> things were. She didn't really appreciate what the 'red
> mud' was that people used to talk about. We certainly got
> an opportunity to see what that was like the other day.[3]

Ted described going back to where his tent lines were in
Nui Dat as 'fantastic', but he tempered that reaction by
saying it was good 'just to be back there with people who'd
been there at the time, and realise that we all came out of
it pretty well'.[4] Having been an RMO and seeing and

dealing intimately with the debris and casualties of war is fairly sobering, and Ted reflected on that side of what the pilgrimage meant to him:

> I was with a lot of blokes when they died, obviously, being the doctor. And you just wonder about what they gave their lives for. But yes, it does make you think about all that and it also makes you think about how lucky we are all here.[5]

The highlight for Ted was going back to Long Tan and standing in the rubber. He had been involved in treating casualties from the evening before and after the battle, and the significance of the Long Tan Cross is definitely not lost on him. As he said, 'It meant a lot.' Ted also took part in Medcaps out to villages like Xuyen Moc, Binh Gia and Hoa Long, and for the medico they were highlights of the trip he says he will always cherish. Doctors take the Hippocratic Oath to treat their fellow man regardless of whose side of the conflict they may be on.[6] This was brought home to Ted when he returned to Long Hai and met the former enemy, as he recalled:

> I thought that was great. They were just the same as us. I didn't feel particularly uncomfortable about treating the enemy wounded. In fact, I thought they deserved to be treated well. And they were [treated well] by our guys.[7]

Ted believes that returning veterans should be aware that Viet Nam is not as easy a place to visit as when 'we were soldiers once and young', adding that veterans should 'just make sure that they are reasonably healthy'. Ted believes that returning is very much an individual choice, but one that he'd recommend: 'I'd say, "Go. Go and bloody do it." And go and do it now. Don't wait another five years.'[8]

Peter Isaacs is always a deep thinker and often talked about the political side of the conflict (not a recommended subject a lot of the time), but he thought that his return visit had altered his views:

> I thought, probably until this trip, that we were right to have participated in the war. I'm not so sure now, but at the time I certainly thought we were right. I felt the loss of our 25 men quite deeply . . . I don't know, I'm confused, but like soldiers before us, we did our duty, we served, and that is good enough for me now.[9]

For Peter, the highlight of his pilgrimage was 'meeting my comrades again'. Comradeship means much to Peter, who lives and works on the other side of the globe, so for him it was more about being with his mates rather than the symbolism of a pilgrimage. He enjoyed his trip, had no regrets about it, but added: 'I would never have come alone. And I'll not come again. I have satisfied my curiosity . . . absolutely.'

Peter views the development of Viet Nam as being ugly, but appreciates the tenacity of the people: 'Looking at the faces of those kids at Binh Gia: they are the future. It's their grandfathers on one side that I have great admiration for . . . The ARVN soldiers who fought gallantly in many instances.'[10]

Ben Morris was glad that he and his second wife Jenny made the effort, even though he had been back twice

before and Jenny had to return early due to work commitments. He wasn't sure if veterans should come back alone
as they might not be able to get clearances if travelling
singly, and reflected on the benefit of having his wife with
him on the pilgrimage. He appreciated:

> just being able to talk to Jenny about a lot of things that
> I haven't been able to in the past. She's gone home with
> a lot more wisdom about that particular side of things.
> Having Jenny being able to see other people and saying,
> 'Oh, that's what you're talking about . . . Now I understand
> where you're coming from.' So from the relationship
> point, it was great.[11]

Ben was also worried whether leaving a return trip for
'something to do later' would be wise:

> The big problem I see for groups coming here in the
> future, if they don't do it in the next five years, most of
> what we know and see is going to be totally obliterated.
> And you've got to realise that Vung Tau to Ba Ria is now
> one long big conurbation. And there's people now living
> where there were no people . . . Nui Dat hill may not be
> there in five years.[12]

Cattle breeder and beef baron Fred Pfitzner had his tongue
firmly in his cheek when he said he was glad he came on
the 5 RAR pilgrimage because it got him out of the calving
on his New South Wales property just outside Canberra. He
was serious, though, when he remarked that the highlight
for him was 'going to Long Tan'. Fred served as the Director
of Infantry during his career, and remains strongly imbued

with the regimental spirit. He explained that Long Tan was so important:

> because of its significance to the regiment in particular—
> although I wasn't at or in any way involved in the battle. It
> is just a place of pilgrimage for members of the regiment.
> All wars are like that. There's one point of commemor-
> ation of campaigns or major battles. There's not little bits
> of skirmishes here and there. So that's one point and it's
> the appropriate point. And if we were never allowed back
> to the Balmoral and Coral areas it wouldn't really matter
> because the Regiment's memorial is there.[13]

Fred enjoyed the camaraderie of the journey back and loved having a beer with his mates at the end of a day's touring. It refreshed him, and he said, 'just reacting with other people reminds you of things you've forgotten'. Fred's only regret was that his wife Helen was not able to join him because of her demanding work commitments, but Fred vowed, 'I'll come back some other time and go to the areas in the central highlands when I came over in 1965.'

What impressed Fred was the manner in which the Vietnamese people have got on with rebuilding their country since the war:

> Because they've got one government that's going to be
> here forever, in their view, and they're taking the long-
> term view that politically our governments never do and
> they seem to have a blueprint for the future. And that's
> evident, I think. And good luck to them. And once they

get the oil and gas sorted out, I mean, you'd expect it'll boom. It would have been pretty sad if it hadn't moved on.[14]

Like Fred, Ron Shambrook was extremely glad that he came, and he also was *sans* wife as his good lady fell ill just prior to the trip and couldn't travel. She insisted Ron make the pilgrimage with the 5 RAR men, because 'she knew how much it meant to me', Ron said wistfully.

Ron's highlights were that he 'got to identify some of the areas where we served. It brought back to me a lot of memories that perhaps had been put away in my mind somewhere.' The fellowship was good for Ron as well: 'Just talking to the other people on tour—that would trigger an item or a period of time, and I've enjoyed that very much indeed.' Ron found the day at An Nhut especially emotional.

> That was a very gut-wrenching day for me because I'd been relieving for some ten days as the SO3 officer at Task Force Headquarters. I took over Charlie Company in the field. Within half an hour of that, Bravo Company drove past. Having been 2IC Bravo Company for quite some time, we identified each other and made all sorts of comments and remarks to each other as they drove past. And not too many minutes later down the track there was this loud noise, puff of quite black smoke that went into the air. And dust. And of course that was the loss of many of my close friends in Bravo Company.[15]

John Taske believed that the pilgrimage had lived up to expectations. 'It was a great trip and well worthwhile.' The dramatic and massive changes in the urban development and basic infrastructure didn't faze him. As he said:

> We could hardly recognise anything. One pleasant surprise was that where I spent six months in about 100 metres by 400 metres in the first six months of that tour in the Nui Dat rubber plantation, it was still like it was.[16]

John has remarried since he served in Viet Nam, and thought it was a great idea that his wife Tina accompanied him. 'This gave her a very good insight into that part of my life, which is important.' Interestingly, John said he 'wouldn't have come back on my own and gone through battlefields. I might have come back to go through the rest of the country ... But no, I would not have gone to the battlefields.'[17]

Even though he was instrumental in getting the 5 RAR pilgrimage off the ground, Roger Wainwright expressed the feeling before he came that he wasn't sure if the pilgrimage was going to be good or bad for him, but this was the best way to find out—regardless. Afterwards he said he was 'very pleased and glad' he had done the trip. He reflected on what his group had achieved:

> There were a few of the things that I really wanted to see, and I think we've done that. And I think the other thing is that down the track we've come back to what I see is a very progressive country. Just to see the infrastructure and things like that which are happening—this country's going to go a long way.[18]

Coming back with his wife of 36 years, Tina, was important to Roger, 'because over many years she's been to reunions, and she comes along and hears all the stories'. Tina was present during the interview and nodded her head vigorously, adding, 'I have heard them all!' Roger continued, 'What Tina has seen now, she's seen first hand, and I think she'll understand a little more about the "warries" that we tend to spin at these reunions.'

But Roger got more out of his trip back than just having a more knowledgeable partner; for him the main thing was being with his fellow soldiers. Roger did not wish to sound elitist, but explained why they had an officer-only group:

> [It was] the camaraderie, the spirit, the feeling between us. This trip was initiated when we laid up the battalion colours in Wagga in April last year [2004]. And the reason we did that was because we had about 17 officers from the first tour turn up from all over the country just to lay up the colours. And that shows the bond that we've got between us. It's stayed strong to this day, and that's why.[19]

Dr Tony White was grinning when asked if he had enjoyed his pilgrimage with his family. 'I'm thrilled,' he said. 'I think it's been just wonderful.' One of Tony's highlights was revisiting his old tent lines:

> Particularly for me the 5 RAR battalion site was very evocative. And to be confident of the exact locations within a matter of metres of the battalion headquarters, and my RAP [regimental aid post], and even to sort of having an intelligent guess as to where my tent was. That was a very emotional sort of moment. It's been superb.[20]

Returning with his wife and son to where he served on active service was important to Tony. He explained:

> I'm very pleased and very proud. Because I think when there's some big event in somebody's life who's dear to you and it's just a sort of cloudy thing ... it makes the whole thing a lot more real and clear and less of a mystery. And so I'm very grateful they came.[21]

Another great moment for Tony was the memorial service in the rubber at Nui Dat. He continued:

> And I thought that little service at Tiger Pad was just spot on ... There we were on that patch of real estate where we'd spent that time, and just doing our duty to those blokes who didn't make it back. And I think they would be grateful for that. And the whole Battalion Association would be grateful for that. That's a sort of chunk of my past which it's nice to be able to visit and commemorate in some way.[22]

The partners

It is one thing for servicemen who have worked together to get together, but for their partners it can be daunting knowing they are going to spend the next couple of weeks touring with a group they might hardly know. Ted Heffernan's wife Joy was also a little worried about their reception by the Vietnamese, but those concerns were soon dispelled: 'I found the Vietnamese people to be very, very friendly,' she said. 'And yes, I've been very impressed with

the country. It is beautiful.' Coming to Viet Nam from
Melbourne was a bit tough for Joy at first.

> We left a cold climate and when we came here it was
> very, very hot. And so I didn't expect it to be so—[even]
> having lived in Singapore and Malaysia for three years.
> Having just spent a week in Singapore a couple of months
> ago, you'd think I would have expected the humidity. But
> in fact it was a lot hotter than I expected, and just visiting
> the areas in the heat was a little bit hard at times.[23]

Joy may have been finding the heat and humidity hard
but it certainly didn't stop her enjoying herself and the
company of the other partners on the trip. Before downing
a bottle of champagne one evening by the pool in Vung Tau
she confided in me that she 'didn't drink', so she was
obviously on a rehydration program that only included
French alcoholic beverages. Joy sheepishly admitted:

> Well, it was a lot of fun. And it was a great bonding of all
> the ladies . . . And it was great that we were all sort of
> fit women together and we were able to cope with the
> experience. I enjoyed all that. I thought it was a great
> adventure.[24]

Tina Wainwright was in on the ground floor of the planning and execution of the 5 RAR pilgrimage because her
husband Roger is president of the battalion association
and was a chief organiser of the officers' trip. Tina was
'very glad' that she accompanied Roger, because 'it's just
a fascinating country. It's a lovely country. And I think it's
terrific to see the development.' Tina's highlights were:

the three ceremonies. It's rather lovely to be able to do it in this country for those men [who died]. The three: Long Tan, the Bourne incident [An Nhut] and Tiger Pad. Probably because of what they meant to Roger.[25]

When the group visited Nui Dat, it rained right on cue as they were having a picnic lunch. Everyone just stood out in the rain and ate their lunch. That made an impression on Tina, who reflected:

You can visualise or you can have a small comprehension [as] somebody who's never been in a war. You can at least imagine. But seeing the ground was important. You can [look at] photographs, but the smells, and looking, and all the senses [make it real].[26]

John Taske's wife Tina said of her trip, 'I would not have missed it for the world; coming with no expectations; going home with a feeling of warmth, love, and respect more than anything.' When asked to elaborate, Tina explained she felt:

respect firstly for the Australian soldiers who fought here; secondly I have a huge respect for the Vietnamese people, which I didn't have before I came. I had never been to an Asian country before—it was difficult for me because I didn't know what to expect—but I would not have missed it for the world. I am a seasoned traveller, but not to Asian countries, and it was difficult for me in the first instance, but I can honestly say now that it was fantastic.[27]

Tina was unable to accompany her husband John on the second half of the pilgrimage, which was really an extended R&R for the touring party, but she said there were several highlights of her trip:

> One was with Roger [Wainwright] when he showed me a photograph and he said, 'These are my men, this photograph was taken about ten minutes before these men were killed.' I just stopped, I couldn't think . . . everything just stopped. And then we went to the place where these men were killed and I felt an enormous loss, an enormous loss. I can't describe it any other way but it was just this huge loss. For life, for family, for everyone there more than anything. Secondly standing at the memorial for the Australian soldiers in the rubber at Long Tan. Walking through the rubber trees; I walked alone for a little while and tried to imagine, I wanted to imagine what it was like with the noise, the guns, bombs and smoke—people with ripped and torn flesh. It crippled my brain and I couldn't. To me it was very moving and once again I felt an enormous amount of respect for these men. And I think there was another moment too when Paul [Greenhalgh] talked about The Horseshoe area and Fort Wendy and I thought, God this is so fantastic, here was a man who was desperate to get home and all he could think about was the woman he loved at home, but here he was doing what he had to do and he managed to mix the two quite nicely until he didn't like the outcome for him. I thought it was really, really nice; it was so lovely to watch Wendy come back with Paul and be part of something that was 39 years ago, which is as strong today as it was then.[28]

When asked how she felt as a woman who had not known her husband when he was in Viet Nam on active service, and as a second wife trying to fit in, Tina was straight-forward in her reply:

> This was a great group, there was no doubt about it. There was no animosity; there were no great moments of tension as you often find in groups. This was a group of people who just bonded, they just melded together and it was just lovely. I adored the women, the ladies were sensational; the men were just gorgeous. The only thing about the bus was that there was no toilet [laughs]. That's all.[29]

And from a woman who brought a new meaning to the words 'retail therapy' and who looked like she could take to the catwalk on any given day in the heat and humidity of Viet Nam and still knock the socks off anyone watching, she added:

> It was fantastic. I would recommend it to any woman who has doubts, or any partner who has doubts about what their husband/partner did or whatever, I heartily recommend that you bring your partner because it will bring you closer together and I think that is what it has actually done for me—it has made me understand my husband more.[30]

Wendy Greenhalgh was asked what she took home from the pilgrimage and replied a little warily, watching her husband's reactions:

I'm only looking at it [as] the wife of Paul, and I'm just
so pleased that we're here and it worked out and everything was happy. And I think he's got something out of
it. I think he's a bit more forgiving. Maybe. But things
have come together and I just believe we've had a bit of
completion here.[31]

Wendy found the trip remarkable for many reasons, but
was especially moved by the Memorial Cross at Long Tan:

I found it incredibly sad there, that all those Viet Cong
are also dead. I felt really depressed about war. I put my
anti-war hat on definitely then. It just all seemed so sad
that it ever happened. All those dead bodies and the poor
mothers and sisters and brothers who will never
ever know where their kin is buried.[32]

Doffy White has been married to her doctor husband Tony
since 1968 and has heard the stories—which didn't get
much airing until only a few years ago—and with their son
Rupert enjoyed the trip immensely. Doffy thought the
highlights were:

being part of a group like this—I think it's an absolute
privilege because you don't often get to be with a group
like that who are talking about what happened to their
lives and they're quite open. I think there was an openness
there that I felt. Being part of that group I thought was
very special, and I felt very honoured to be included. And
I think seeing where Tony served, that was also very
special.[33]

After visiting where her husband had toiled as the unit doctor, Doffy admitted she hadn't thought of some of the little things that are hardly ever mentioned about being in a war zone.

> What I hadn't appreciated was the privations that they must have had: the rain, the constant heat and humidity, ants crawling up your legs, the tiny little bugs that would be crawling in and out of your clothes, and the fact that you were constantly wet. Someone mentioned that they once went for about 30 days without changing their clothes and as they dried out the next lot of rain would come. When you listen to all the stories back home, [the men] really don't talk about those sort of things—and from a female's perspective I found that horrendous, I mean how could you cope? And the other thing I found [was] that the beauty in the rubber was mesmerising. I remember looking down that cathedral of rubber trees and the canopy underneath; I thought it was exquisitely beautiful and yet spooky. I found the combination of those two aspects really extraordinary.[34]

Doffy thought that the memory she would be taking from Viet Nam would probably sound 'off to left field a little bit':

> [It was] just driving down those village tracks and looking at all the villages. And this is nearly 40 years later on [since the war]. And if this is what it's like now, imagining how it would have been—it must have been much more primitive then. Here are these people hammering nails on

the sort of side walk, hammering down buildings with sledge hammers and whatever. And I think here is this poor community on a little strip of land and yet they beat the combined might of America and its Allies. And I think ... as a grandparent now, what can we learn? We should teach our children about surviving in the future. And I think that's what I'll take back.[35]

The children

Rupert White accompanied his parents on the 5 RAR pilgrimage when he was 34 years old. Here are some of his thoughts on the journey:

My expectations were [that it would be] almost like wandering through a museum, that is how I thought it was going to go. 'This is where this happened, this is where that happened.' It turned out to be a bit more than that. I got a few good war stories out of the old boys which was great. And John Taske tells a really great story about showering in the camp before the duck boards were down and the red mud and that sort of thing—you hear about the guns and the bullets and the deaths, but you don't really hear about day to day life in Nui Dat or out on patrol so much. And so just those little stories added a thousand shades of colour to the way I see it now. And also the rain in the rubber, and the insects biting our feet while we were doing the memorial service. And the mud. Whereas before I saw photos, now I've got a real feel of what it must have been like.[36]

Rupert said the trip had given him a better understanding of what his father Tony had experienced, and had fulfilled his expectations 'and more so'. He admitted he was a little apprehensive at first, but said that feeling quickly dissipated.

> I thought I'd better be on my best behaviour, and all these guys here—it was like touring with a rugby squad or something. You know, there were jokes left, right and centre and all that sort of stuff. It was great ... They've obviously got a very good relationship from just that one year in Viet Nam. I'm really glad I came. I was very honoured to get the invitation.[37]

There was no shortage of war stories on the tour bus or whenever the group stopped at a battle site, museum or other place of interest. Rupert remarked:

> Another thing that I've got from the whole thing was just ... actually seeing people describing amongst themselves when people have been killed whom they knew, or Gary [McKay] getting blasted in the arm and you hear of someone being shot and injured. And that's—okay, that's a bad thing. But behind each of those stories it actually doesn't end there. Then it can be two years or five years of rehabilitation. And I think, going forward from there, I have a greater respect or understanding of thousands of casualties in Gallipoli and places like that. There is actually a little person behind each of those statistics.[38]

So what would Rupert leave Viet Nam with as his greatest impression?

I think again the biggest thing I'll take back is just the mateship, the banter on the bus. I always think that your generals and all your captains and your majors—my assumption is that they're going to be hard arses, you know, very tough. But you see Paul out there and he's naming 'Fort Wendy' and that sort of thing. And Roger's such a lovely quiet guy (for an infantryman). I think that's a good impression of mateship and that's the thing I'll take away with me for sure.[39]

Tony White was listening as his son spoke, and then offered another observation on how children of war veterans may react on a visit to Viet Nam: 'I think it depends a lot on whether they've had the whole Viet Nam thing rammed down their throat or not.' When asked to clarify that remark Tony added, 'I think of some families where the kids and spouses have overdosed on it and for them it would just be piling another toxin on a bad life back home.'[40]

My own daughter, Kelly, was 21 when she accompanied me to Viet Nam on a research trip in 2002. I would like to share here her reflections on that visit and what she came away with. This was her unedited response:

Whilst I was initially apprehensive at joining a whole group of other veterans (besides my father), this feeling soon proved to be completely unfounded, as I was made exceptionally welcome and soon made some lovely friends. It soon became apparent that while revisiting Viet Nam is a very personal and individual experience for each veteran, having the support network of their spouses and other returning veterans was invaluable in helping them through this sometimes confronting and difficult experience. However, it wasn't all so emotional, and having people with similar experiences with whom to share memories, stories and lots of laughs made for a very fun and exciting atmosphere. The drinks and the anecdotes flowed freely and by the end of our tour firm friendships were forged.

As the daughter of a Viet Nam veteran and career Army officer of 30 years, my youth was filled with hundreds of Viet Nam and military anecdotes. 'Army' was so ingrained in my father that it seemed to infiltrate all aspects of his personality and our lives. There is at least one Viet Nam story that can be related to nearly every possible everyday situation (the ones about chillies and giant spiders among my personal favourites), and so, like many other 'Army brats', Viet Nam is something I thought I understood. My father's experience with war was part of our everyday lives and was something I took very much for granted.

All this changed on going to Viet Nam with my father. I learned very quickly that the anecdotes of my childhood were just that—stories. Minute snapshots of the 'PG' version of war; the lighter moments in a war that was anything but. What I thought I knew about the Viet Nam War didn't even come close to scratching the surface of what the Viet Nam experience really was all about for my father and his fellow veterans.

Whilst every day of my trip was a new and exciting discovery, there were three particularly standout moments that really defined for me what it must have been like for my father in Viet Nam. The first was a visit to the War Remnants Museum. Even someone not connected to a veteran could not help but be moved by the highly emotive and confronting images on display here. My father warned me before entering that some of the photographs would be graphic, but nothing could have prepared me for the shock of what I saw. I realised straight away that the 'War Remnants Museum' could not have been more aptly named. Wounded men crying in agony, surgeons up to their elbows in gore, and the foetuses of babies deformed in utero as a result of their mothers' exposure to Agent Orange are memories that will stay with me always as a constant reminder of the futility of war.

The second event that helped deepen my understanding was visiting the site of the Memorial Cross for the Battle of Long Tan. It was a very hot and humid day as we all sat among the rubber trees listening to my father deliver a blow-by-blow account of the battle. The experience was incredibly chilling. The bravery and the strength of the Australian soldiers against such incredible odds was mind-blowing, and the sense of overwhelming pride and respect I felt for these men and all other veterans is one I will carry with me always.

The third moment came much more unexpectedly, but really made me confront the full gravity of what my father felt, and continues to live with today. Whilst walking through the 'jungle' to the site of the Cu Chi tunnels, one of the veterans suddenly froze. He looked very shaken, and I asked my father what was wrong. He explained that the uniform worn by the staff at Cu Chi was very similar to the black pyjama-style uniforms worn by the Viet Cong during the war. Our friend, on his first return trip to Viet Nam, had just caught a glimpse of one of the staff through the jungle. For him it was like being in a time warp. The humidity, the jungle and then sighting 'the enemy' through the trees transported him back, and the adrenaline and fear were, once again, very real.

As we walked on, the reality of how it must have felt came crashing down on me. A cold shiver ran down my spine as I tried to comprehend how it must have felt really to be there. To kill or be killed. The feeling was positively overwhelming and to finally understand that this was a reality that my father actually lived through was as terrifying as it was humbling.

I have always considered myself a 'Daddy's girl' and have always loved, respected and admired my father. But after going to Viet Nam with him, I felt I finally understood him a little better. I will never again take for granted or dismiss what he went through. His anecdotes are not 'just another Viet Nam story'; they were real, and only a tiny part of the montage of his experience. The sadness and pain I feel for my father because of what he went through is overshadowed only by the immense feeling of pride and respect I feel for the man it made him become.

Viet Nam for me was an incredible experience. The sensory overload was intoxicating. The country was as beautiful as it was scarred. Everywhere you look it seems you are confronted by a visual oxymoron. Lotus blossoms and duck ponds in bomb craters; battle wounds on smiling faces; and happiness in the midst of poverty. Girls dressed in beautiful spotless, white silk *ao dais* riding clapped-out bikes on pot-holed dusty roads. It is a country of contradiction, and a place I will never forget.[41]

EPILOGUE

This book has attempted to give the veteran who is contemplating returning to Viet Nam an idea of what they could expect and how they might prepare for their journey, whether it be a pilgrimage or simply a holiday visit as a tourist, and has shared some insights and recommendations from those who have been there and done it.

Whether or not pilgrimages to Viet Nam can and will continue is something only time will tell. Garry Adams took an optimistic view, remarking: 'Hopefully as time comes to pass there will be more and more young ones coming to have a look at the places where their fathers fought.'[1]

Not all veterans who return to Viet Nam find it a positive experience. Those who visit hoping to see familiar sights and well-known ground in order to confirm their memories are often bitterly disappointed. Few signs of the Australian presence remain. The Task Force base at Nui Dat was stripped of all remaining materials by locals shortly after the Australians withdrew. The remaining concrete strip of the former Luscombe Field is now a street surrounded by local dwellings. At the site of the former logistics base at Vung Tau there are few signs of the Badcoe

Recreation club, where Australian soldiers spent their time recovering from injury and illness. Much of the countryside they spent so much time patrolling has also changed—now developed in a variety of ways.

For those seeking to make sense of the chaos of their memories, not being able to see the ground as it was then only adds to their sense of confusion. Not being able to find visual signs of their presence can also make some veterans feel as if their efforts were in vain. For others, though, the lack of war remnants is a positive sign. They see that the country has moved on and are happy that the country and its people, in the south at least, appear to be thriving. Relatives of veterans also have varying reactions to their visits. Those who travelled in the 1980s and early 90s often found travel in Viet Nam difficult and un-comfortable, and Viet Nam was not a place to which they would readily return. Most have been happy, though, to be able to provide emotional support when it was needed, and have found the trip worthwhile.

On 21 May 1970, a young Australian soldier, Assault Pioneer Graham Edwards, stepped on a mine in South Viet Nam. Many of the so-called 'Jumping Jack' M-16 mines deployed by the Viet Cong against South Vietnamese and Allied soldiers had been lifted from the Australians' own barrier minefield, and were causing widespread death and injury. Pioneer Edwards survived the blast, but with both legs amputated he now relies on a wheelchair for mobility. In May 1990, twenty years after that blast, Graham Edwards, who was by then a Western Australian Member of the Legislative Assembly, went back to Viet Nam. His aim in returning was, in his words, 'to sort out the ghosts'. With the aid of a former Viet Cong platoon commander, Edwards was able to locate the site of the explosion which changed his life. Having confronted his ghosts he returned to Australia, determined to help the disabled and other Viet Nam veterans. As a federal Member of Parliament Graham Edwards has been able to fulfil his goals.

There are many stories like that of Graham Edwards. Paul Murphy was another veteran who went back to Viet Nam in 1990; he was so shocked by the poverty he found there that he vowed to return and help in some way. Four years later he went back to Viet Nam, signed a memorandum of understanding with the local government, and formed the Australian Veterans Vietnam Reconstruction Group (AVVRG). The group has since undertaken numerous projects to help the people of the former Phuoc Tuy Province, raising well over a million dollars in aid in the last ten years. As well, the AVVRG has been responsible for the recent refurbishment of the Long Tan Memorial Cross site.[2]

In 1996, veterans' pilgrimages to Viet Nam entered the public sphere. In August that year a group of veterans and widows, accompanied by the Deputy Prime Minister, Tim Fischer, and the Minister for Veterans Affairs, Bruce Scott, participated in an official pilgrimage to Viet Nam to mark the thirtieth anniversary of the battle of Long Tan. I was the official historian on that trip, standing in for the then seriously ill historian, the late Ian McNeill. Although time was given for personal remembrance and commemoration, especially at Terandak Military Cemetery in Malaysia, formal ceremonies at various locations set the tone for the tour.

The visit was seen as highly significant for the development of the relationship between Australia and Viet Nam and was promoted as a sign that both sides had moved on from the past. While recognising this, during a speech at Nui Dat Tim Fischer conceded: 'We must acknowledge that Vietnam is still recent history. And if past enmities have died, for many on both sides the scars understandably remain.'[3]

Long Tan survivor Jim Richmond faced his own ghosts during the tour when he presented a commemorative plaque to another Long Tan survivor, from the other side. He saw the pilgrimage as a chance for reconciliation. 'It doesn't really matter now,' he said beforehand. 'What happened, happened. If there was a bloke from Long Tan [there] I'd have a beer with him, ex-soldier to ex-soldier.'[4] Such sentiments are common among pilgrims, and are a sign that they are coming to terms with their Viet Nam experience.

Historian Libby Stewart tackled the issue of the future of pilgrimages to Viet Nam. She said in an address to the University of Newcastle:

It is possible that they will start to wane as veterans become too old to travel. The lack of war graves means that the children of veterans won't have a particular point of reference for their travels, and the changed landscape means that their father's descriptions will mean little to them. Despite these things, I don't believe that Viet Nam will cease to be a place of remembrance for Australians. As we achieve a greater understanding of that war and what it meant for its veterans, the impulses that have sent Australians all over the world to pay tribute to Australian war dead will continue to extend to Viet Nam.[5]

Garry Adams agrees, noting that there is a growing interest among young Australians about our involvement in the war. Each year he sees more of them making the effort to participate in important events held on Anzac Day and Viet Nam Veterans Day at the Long Tan Memorial Cross.

Perhaps their initial rejection by society has created a greater need among Viet Nam veterans to return to their battlefields and ensure that the dead are remembered. Their children will no doubt continue this legacy.

APPENDIX: POST TRAUMATIC STRESS DISORDER

Reproduced with permission from the *Diagnostic and Statistical Manual of Mental Disorders*, 4th edition, published by the American Psychiatric Association, Washington, DC, 2000, pp. 463–6. This text is used as the basis for Australian psychiatry in the examination, diagnosis and treatment of PTSD.

Diagnostic features

There are several reasons why people become affected with Post Traumatic Stress Disorder (PTSD). These causes are clinically referred to as diagnostic features. The essential feature of PTSD is the development of characteristic symptoms following exposure to an extreme traumatic stressor involving direct personal experience of an event that involves actual or threatened death or serious injury, or other threat to one's physical integrity; or witnessing an event that involves death, injury, or a threat to the physical integrity of another person.

The person's response to the event must involve intense fear, helplessness, or horror. The characteristic symptoms resulting from the exposure to the extreme trauma include persistent re-experiencing of the traumatic event, persistent avoidance of stimuli associated with the trauma and numbing of general responsiveness and persistent symptoms of increased arousal. The full symptom picture must be present for more than 1 month and the disturbance must cause clinically significant distress or impairments in social, occupational, or other important areas of functioning.

It is accepted that soldiers in combat will be exposed at some time to stressors that can lead to PTSD. It is not an automatic given that every soldier will be impaired with PTSD. It is not only those in the front line—the 'bayonets' of a military unit—that will be affected in war. What are referred to as 'witnessed events' can include, but are not limited to, observing the serious injury or unnatural death of another person owing to violent assault, accident, war, or disaster or unexpectedly witnessing a dead body or body parts. The disorder may be especially severe or long lasting when the stressor is of human design (e.g. torture, rape). The likelihood of developing this disorder may increase as the intensity of and physical proximity to the stressor increase.

Recurring dreams and flashbacks

The traumatic event can be re-experienced in various ways. Commonly the person has recurrent and intrusive recollections of the event or recurrent or distressing dreams during which the event can be replayed or otherwise represented.

In rare instances, the person experiences dissociative states that last from a few seconds to several hours, or even days, during which components of the event are relived and the person behaves as though experiencing the event at that moment. These episodes, often referred to as 'flashbacks', are typically brief but can be associated with prolonged distress and heightened arousal.

Distress

Intense psychological distress or physiological reactivity [crying, over-reaction and non-reaction to events around them] often occurs when the person is exposed to triggering events that resemble or symbolise an aspect of the traumatic event [e.g. anniversaries of the traumatic event; hot, humid weather for combat veterans from Viet Nam; movies depicting events similar to those witnessed].

Avoidance of stimuli

Sufferers of PTSD will go to extremes to avoid the stimuli that has brought about their disorder and make efforts to persistently avoid thoughts, feelings, or conversations about the traumatic event and to avoid activities, situations, or people who arouse recollections of it. This avoidance of reminders may include amnesia for an important aspect of the traumatic event. This is often referred to as 'psychic numbing' or 'emotional anaesthesia' and usually begins soon after the traumatic event. Veterans may complain of having markedly diminished interest or participation in previously enjoyed activities, of feeling detached or estranged from other people, or of having markedly reduced ability to feel emotions (especially those associated with intimacy, tenderness and sexuality). The individual may have a sense of a foreshortened future (e.g. not expecting to have a career, marriage, children, or a normal life span).

Symptoms

Those with PTSD have persistent symptoms of anxiety or increased arousal that were not present before the trauma. The symptoms may include difficulty falling or staying asleep that may be owing to recurrent nightmares during which the traumatic event is relived, hypervigilance (e.g. locking all the doors and windows in the house before retiring), and exaggerated startle response. Some individuals report irritability or outbursts of anger (e.g. road rage, over-reacting to minor annoyances), or difficulty concentrating or completing tasks.

Specifiers or levels of PTSD

It is recognised that there are three levels or specifiers used to specify the onset and duration of the symptoms of PTSD:

1 *Acute.* This specifier should be used when the duration of the symptom is less than 3 months.
2 *Chronic.* This specifier should be used when the symptoms last 3 months or longer.
3 *With Delayed Onset.* This specifier indicates that at least 6 months have passed between the traumatic event and the onset of the symptoms.

Associated descriptive features and mental disorders

Individuals with PTSD may describe painful guilt feelings about surviving when others did not survive or about the things they had to do to survive. Avoidance patterns may interfere with interpersonal relationships and lead to marital conflict, divorce or loss of job. Apart from self-destructive and anti-social or impulsive behaviour, some individuals feel shame, despair, or hopelessness, hostility and a change of previous personality characteristics. PTSD is associated with increased rates of Major Depressive Disorder, Substance-Related Disorders, Panic Disorder, Agoraphobia, Obsessive-Compulsive Disorder, Generalised Anxiety Disorder, Social Phobia, Specific Phobia and Bipolar Disorder. These disorders can either precede, follow, or emerge concurrently with the onset of PTSD.

Prevalence in combat veterans

Community-based studies in the United States of America reveal a lifetime prevalence for PTSD of approximately

8 per cent of the adult population. Studies of at-risk individuals (i.e. groups exposed to specific trauma incidents) yield variable findings, with highest rates (ranging between one-third and more than half of those exposed) found among groups such as combat veterans and those subjected to politically motivated internment and genocide.

When does it strike?

Post Traumatic Stress Disorder is not related to the age of the individual. Symptoms usually begin within the first 3 months after the trauma, although there may be a delay of months, or even years, before symptoms appear. Frequently, a person's reaction to a trauma initially meets criteria for Acute Stress Disorder in the immediate aftermath of the trauma. Duration of the symptoms varies, with complete recovery occurring within 3 months in approximately half of the cases, with many others having persisting symptoms for longer than 12 months after the trauma. Symptom reactivation may occur in response to reminders of the original trauma, life stressors, or new traumatic events.

GLOSSARY

1 ALSG	1st Australian Logistic Support Group, based at Vung Tau
1 ARU	1st Australian Reinforcement Unit, based at Nui Dat
1 ATF	1st Australian Task Force, based at Nui Dat
2IC	second-in-command
AATTV	Australian Army Training Team Vietnam
AK-47	7.62-mm, automatic Kalishnikov assault rifle
Anzac	Australian and New Zealand Army Corps
ARA	Australian Regular Army
armoured personnel carrier	the M113, a 10-tonne, tracked vehicle
ARVN	Army of the Republic of Viet Nam, the South Vietnamese Regular army
ATF	Australian Task Force, Nui Dat
avgas	aviation gasoline
B-52	strategic US jet bomber
base wallah	a soldier who works in a base or rear area
BHQ	Battalion Headquarters
C-117	a Super DC-3, twin-engined, 24-seater transport aircraft
C-123	Provider, a twin-engined, short-range, tactical transport aircraft

C-130	Hercules, a four-engined, medium-range transport aircraft
Caribou	twin-engined, De Haviland RAAF short-haul transport aircraft
Chinook	CH-47, twin-rotor, medium-lift helicopter
Claymore mine	M18A-1, Claymore, a directional anti-personnel mine that contained 1.25 pounds of HE (high explosive) and 500 steel ball bearings
CMF	Citizen Military Forces, once called Militia, the forerunners to today's Army Reserve
CO	Commanding Officer, usually a lieutenant colonel in rank
CP	Command Post
D 445	a Viet Cong *Local Force* battalion that operated in Phuoc Tuy Province
Dentcaps	dental civil aid projects/programs conducted under the Army's Civil Affairs program in Vietnamese outlying villages
DMZ	demilitarised zone
Dustoff	dedicated helicopter for casualty evacuation
F-4	Phantom jet bomber
FTD	Full-time duty; reservist soldiers who served full time in the ARA
GPS	Global Positioning System, a satellite-based navigation aid
grunt	slang for infantryman
HMAS	Her Majesty's Australian Ship, Royal Australian Navy
HQ	headquarters
J	jungle

LZ	landing zone
M-16 mine	'Jumping Jack', an anti-personnel mine that once tripped was blown into the air about a metre before detonating
M-16 rifle	5.56-mm American automatic and semi-automatic rifle
Medcap	medical civil aid projects/programs conducted under the Army's Civil Affairs program in outlying Vietnamese villages
Military Cross	an officers' decoration for gallantry
Military Medal	a soldiers' decoration for bravery
National Service	two-year full-time service, usually in the Army
NCO	Non-Commissioned Officer, soldiers above the rank of Private soldier and below the rank of commissioned officers
NVA	North Vietnamese Army
OC	Officer Commanding, usually a sub-unit commander and major in rank (Aust.) or captain (US) or lieutenant (ARVN)
OTU	the Officer Training Unit at Scheyville, near Sydney: a National Service officer training institution
piastre	the basic currency unit of Viet Nam during the war, now known as the Dong
PIR	Pacific Islands Regiment, the army of Papua New Guinea when under Australia's Protectorate
Pogo	acronym (unsubstantiated) for 'personnel on garrison operations', see base wallah

Portsea	the Officer Cadet School, Portsea, Victoria; a 12-month commissioning course
Post Exchange	a duty-free store and commissary for soldiers
POW	prisoner of war
Psyops	psychological operations, designed to lower enemy morale, and gain support for the Allied forces
PTSD	post traumatic stress disorder
R&C	rest and convalescence leave, a short break from duties taken in Viet Nam
R&R	rest and recuperation (but usually recreation) leave, taken for 5–7 days outside Viet Nam
RAA	Royal Australian Artillery
RAAF	Royal Australian Air Force
RAAMC	Royal Australian Army Medical Corps
RAEME	Royal Australian Electrical and Mechanical Engineers
RAN	Royal Australian Navy
RAP	Regimental Aid Post, a unit's medical centre
RAR	Royal Australian Regiment, straight leg infantry
reo	a reinforcement soldier
RMC	Royal Military College, Duntroon, Canberra
RMO	Regimental Medical Officer, the unit doctor
RQR	Royal Queensland Regiment
RSL	Returned and Services League
SAS	Special Air Service

SEAL	US Navy Special Forces, acronym for Sea Air and Land forces
SLR	7.62-mm, semi-automatic self-loading rifle, also known as the FN
SO3	Staff Officer Grade 3, usually a captain-ranked staff position
SRV	Socialist Republic of Vietnam
Stokes litter	a wire-framed stretcher used to winch casualties into helicopters
TAOR	Tactical Area of Responsibility, an area assigned to a unit or sub-unit to patrol
Tracker Platoon	a group using Labrador dogs to track the enemy, formed out of the Anti-Tank Platoon, which had limited use in the jungles of South Viet Nam
uc dai loi	the formal Vietnamese expression for Australia. Colloquially translated, it refers to the 'Great Continent' or 'Great South Land'
USMC	the United States Marine Corps, the forces from the Department of the US Navy designed to establish a bridgehead on a beach for later military operations by the Army
VC	Viet Cong, a term invented by the Americans in the late 1950s to rename the Communist Viet Minh, which they considered too nationalistic
VD	venereal disease

| Viet Minh | a contraction of *Viet Nam Doc Lap Dong Minh Hoi*, the term applied to the Vietnamese resistance fighters from the First Indochina (French) War |
| Wallaby Airlines | a nickname given to the RAAF 35 Squadron and the Caribou short take-off and landing aircraft, owing to the squadron insignia on the tailplane |

NOTES

Introduction

1 Elizabeth Stewart, 'Return to Vietnam', Paper, University of Newcastle, 2005

2 Ian McNeill, *The Team: Australian Army Advisers in Vietnam 1962–1972*, pp. 128–9

3 Elizabeth Stewart, op. cit.

4 Ibid

5 Ibid

6 'Vietnam is a densely-populated, developing country that in the last 30 years has had to recover from the ravages of war, the loss of financial support from the old Soviet Bloc, and the rigidities of a centrally-planned economy. Substantial progress was achieved from 1986 to 1997 in moving forward from an extremely low level of development and significantly reducing poverty. Growth averaged around 9 percent per year from 1993 to 1997.' Source: *The World Factbook 2007*, www.cia.gov/cia/publications/factbook/geos/vm.html

7 Elizabeth Stewart, op. cit.

8 Ibid

9 Ibid

10 Bruce Davies and Gary McKay, *The Men Who Persevered—The AATTV: The Most Decorated Australian Unit in the Viet Nam War*, Allen & Unwin, Sydney, 2005

11   Gary McKay, *Delta Four—Australian Riflemen in Vietnam*, Allen & Unwin, Sydney, 1996
12   Interview with Garry Adams, Hoi An, SRV, 12 October 2005

Chapter 1 Great expectations

1   Interview with Garry Adams, Hoi An, SRV, 12 October 2005
2   Letter, Steve Campling, 24 December 2005
3   Letter, Derrill De Heer, 17 May 2006
4   Ibid
5   Letter, Bob Hann, 25 July 2006
6   Letter, Garry Heskett, 19 June 2006
7   Ibid
8   Letter, Suzanne Heskett, 16 June 2006
9   Interview with Bill Kromwyk, Mt Gravatt, Qld, 27 February 2006
10   Ibid
11   Ibid
12   Interview with Peter Rogers, Yaroomba, Qld, 12 December 2005
13   Ibid
14   Ibid
15   Ibid
16   Letter, Ian Ryan, 2 May 2006
17   Interview with Garry Adams, 12 October 2005
18   Ibid
19   Ibid
20   Letter, Bob Hann
21   Letter, Steve Campling
22   Letter, Derrill De Heer
23   Letter, Garry Heskett
24   Letter, Ian Ryan
25   Letter, Derrill De Heer

26 Interview with Bill Kromwyk, 27 February 2006
27 Ibid
28 Interview with Peter Rogers, 12 December 2005
29 Gary McKay, *Delta Four—Australian Riflemen in Vietnam*, Allen &
    Unwin, Sydney, 1996, p. 246

Chapter 2 The 5 RAR tour group

1   Interview with Paul Greenhalgh, Canberra, ACT, 20 February
    2005
2   The HMAS *Sydney* was a converted ex-Royal Navy aircraft
    carrier. This 'fast troop transport' ship became known as the
    'Vung Tau Ferry' or 'The Steak and Kidney'.
3   Interview with Paul Greenhalgh, 20 February 2005. In the
    Second World War Chin Peng rose to prominence in the jungles
    of Malaya where many Chinese Malayans were waging a guerrilla
    war against the occupying Japanese. After the war he was elected
    Secretary General of the Communist Party of Malaya and gained
    notoriety for leading an armed insurgency that was responsible
    for the deaths of many civilians. He was exiled from Malaya but
    continued to lead the struggle against British rule.
4   Interview with Paul Greenhalgh, 20 February 2005
5   Citizen Military Forces (now known as the Army Reserve) sol-
    diers and officers could be transferred to the Regular Army on
    what was called Full Time Duty status, abbreviated to FTD—
    usually for a minimum period of twelve months.
6   The Officer Training Unit at Scheyville just outside Sydney was
    established in 1965 to train selected national servicemen as
    officers for the Army. It was a 22-week course and based on
    the twelve-month Regular Army Officer Cadet School (OCS)
    course conducted at Portsea in Victoria. The training is
    described in some detail in my first book, *In Good Company*, Allen
    & Unwin, Sydney, 1987.

7   Interview with Paul Greenhalgh, 20 February 2005
8   Ibid
9   Ibid
10 Ibid
11 Ibid
12 Ibid
13 Ibid
14 Interview with Paul and Wendy Greenhalgh, Hoi An, SRV, 12 October 2005
15 Ibid
16 Prospective medical officers were trained in an Army under-graduate medical program that required a return of service obligation after graduation of at least five years.
17 Interview with Ted and Joy Heffernan, Hoi An, SRV, 11 October 2005
18 Ibid
19 Ibid
20 Interview with Peter Isaacs, Hoi An, SRV, 11 October 2005
21 Ibid
22 Letter, Peter Isaacs, 7 September 2005
23 Ibid
24 Ibid
25 Interview with Ben Morris, Yaroomba, Qld, 8 March 2005
26 Ibid
27 Ibid
28 Ibid
29 Ibid
30 Ibid
31 Ibid
32 Ibid
33 Ibid

34   Ibid

35   Ibid

36   Interview with Ben Morris, Hoi An, SRV, 12 October 2005

37   Interview with Ben Morris, 8 March 2005

38   Interview with Fred Pfitzner, Royalla, NSW, 2 September 2005

39   Ibid

40   Ibid

41   Ibid

42   Ibid

43   The Army infantry battalions underwent several organisational changes after the Second World War as defence planners struggled to come to grips with a shift in alliances and a change in strategic outlook. These changes are discussed in a history of The Royal Australian Regiment, *Duty First*, by Dr David Horner, Allen & Unwin, Sydney, 1990, pp. 134–44.

44   Interview with Ron Shambrook, Brisbane, Qld, 14 July 2005

45   Ibid

46   Ibid

47   Ibid

48   Letter, John Taske, 13 September 2005

49   Interview with John Taske, Hoi An, SRV, 11 October 2005

50   Letter, John Taske

51   Ibid

52   Interview with Tina Taske, Ho Chi Minh City, SRV, 9 October 2005

53   Interview with Roger Wainwright, Canberra, ACT, 15 February 2005

54   Ibid

55   Ibid

56   Ibid

57   Ibid

58 Ibid
59 Interview with Roger and Tina Wainwright, Hoi An, SRV, 11 October 2005
60 Ibid
61 Letter, Tony White, 9 September 2005
62 Ibid
63 Ibid
64 Interview with Tony, Doffy and Rupert White, Ho Chi Minh City, SRV, 9 October 2005
65 Letter, Tony White
66 Ibid
67 Interview with the White family, 9 October 2005
68 Ibid
69 Ibid
70 Ibid
71 Ibid

Chapter 3 Ho Chi Minh City (Saigon) and surrounds

1 Gary McKay, *Australia's Battlefields in Viet Nam*, Allen & Unwin, Sydney, 2004; this book is a tool for those who wish to visit the battlefields where the 1st Australian Task Force units fought during the war. For a more comprehensive guide to the country, the culture and travel-oriented matters, readers should refer to travel guides such as Lonely Planet.
2 Letter, Peter Isaacs, 18 November 2005
3 Interview with Peter Rogers, Yaroomba, Qld, 12 December 2005
4 Letter, Derrill De Heer, 17 May 2006
5 Interview with Ron Shambrook, Brisbane, Qld, 14 July 2005
6 Interview with Peter Rogers, 12 December 2005
7 Gary McKay, *Bullets, Beans & Bandages: Australians at War in Viet Nam*, Allen & Unwin, Sydney, 1999, p. 74

8   Gary McKay, *Bullets, Beans & Bandages*, p. 61

9   Gary McKay, *Bullets, Beans & Bandages*, p. 73. Wallaby Airlines was
    the nickname given to the RAAF 35 Squadron and the Caribou
    short take-off and landing aircraft, owing to the squadron
    insignia on the tailplane.

10 For a full account of the battles, see *The Battle of Coral: Fire Support
    Bases Coral and Balmoral May 1968* by Lex McAulay, Hutchinson,
    Melbourne, 1988.

11 Interview with Peter Rogers, 12 December 2005

Chapter 4 Inside the wire: Nui Dat

1   Interview with Bill Kromwyk, Mt Gravatt, Qld, 27 February
    2006

2   Letter, Derrill De Heer, 17 May 2006. (On 23 November 1969
    and just prior to 9 RAR's departure from South Viet Nam, a
    disgruntled soldier placed an M26 HE grenade into a tent that
    housed Lieutenant Convery and his platoon sergeant. Convery
    was killed in the subsequent explosion.)

3   Letter, Bob Hann, 25 July 2006

4   Letter, Ian Ryan, 2 May 2006

5   Interview with Roger Wainwright, Canberra, ACT, 15 February
    2005

6   Interview with Ron Shambrook, Brisbane, Qld, 14 July 2005

7   Ibid

8   Letter, Peter Isaacs, 18 November 2005

9   Interview with Paul Greenhalgh, Canberra, ACT, 20 February
    2005

10 Interview with Ben Morris, Hoi An, SRV, 12 October 2005

11 Interview with Fred Pfitzner, Hoi An, SRV, 11 October 2005

12 Interview with Peter Rogers, Yaroomba, Qld, 12 December
    2005

13 The Australian Veterans Vietnam Reconstruction Group also
    supports an orphanage in Ba Ria (Phuoc Le) township and has
    been doing so for many years. For more information on their
    activities see their website at http://avvrg.au104.org/.

14 Interview with John Taske, Hoi An, SRV, 11 October 2005

15 Interview with Tony, Doffy and Rupert White, Ho Chi Minh
    City, SRV, 9 October 2005

16 Interview with Rupert White, Vung Tau, SRV, 8 October 2005

17 Interview with Roger and Tina Wainwright, Hoi An, SRV,
    11 October 2005

18 Ibid

Chapter 5 Outside the wire: Phuoc Tuy

1   Interview with Bill Kromwyk, Mt Gravatt, Qld, 27 February
    2006

2   The Regional Forces (formerly the Civil Guard) and the
    Popular Forces (formerly the Self Defence Corps) were South
    Vietnamese militia. The Popular Forces were trained and
    equipped to a lesser level than the Regional Forces.

3   Letter, Garry Heskett, 19 June 2006

4   Interview with Bill Kromwyk, 27 February 2006

5   Operation Hardihood was conducted from 24 May to 12 June
    1966, and involved units from the American 173rd Airborne
    Brigade (Separate) based at Bien Hoa, 5 RAR and elements of
    the future Australian Task Force.

6   Interview with Peter Isaacs, Hoi An, SRV, 11 October 2005

7   Ibid

8   Interview with Paul Greenhalgh, Canberra, ACT, 20 February
    2005

9   Interview with Bill Kromwyk, 27 February 2006

10 Interview with Ben Morris, Hoi An, SRV, 12 October 2005

11   Ibid
12   Interview with Fred Pfitzner, Hoi An, SRV, 11 October 2005
13   Interview with Peter Rogers, Yaroomba, Qld, 12 December 2005
14   Interview with Ron Shambrook, Hoi An, SRV, 12 October 2005
15   Interview with John Taske, Hoi An, SRV, 11 October 2005
16   Interview with Roger Wainwright, Canberra, ACT, 15 February 2005
17   Ibid
18   Ibid
19   Interview with Ron Shambrook, 12 October 2005
20   Interview with Paul Greenhalgh, 20 February 2005
21   Interview with Paul and Wendy Greenhalgh, Hoi An, SRV, 12 October 2005
22   Interview with Fred Pfitzner, Royalla, NSW, 2 September 2005
23   Interview with Roger and Tina Wainwright, Hoi An, SRV, 11 October 2005
24   Interview with John Taske, 11 October 2005
25   Interview with Paul Greenhalgh, 20 February 2005
26   Letter, Derrill De Heer, 17 May 2006
27   Interview with Peter Isaacs, 11 October 2005
28   Interview with Bill Kromwyk, 27 February 2006
29   Interview with Fred Pfitzner, 11 October 2005
30   Ibid
31   Interview with Roger and Tina Wainwright, 11 October 2005
32   Interview with Tony, Doffy and Rupert White, Ho Chi Minh City, SRV, 9 October 2005
33   Robert O'Neill, *Vietnam Task: The 5th Battalion, the Royal Australian Regiment, 1966–67*, Cassell Australia, Melbourne, 1968, pp. 221–6, 228
34   Interview with the White family, 9 October 2005
35   Interview with Roger Wainwright, 15 February 2005
36   Letter, Peter Isaacs, 18 November 2005
37   Interview with Roger Wainwright, 15 February 2005

38 Interview with Peter Rogers, 12 December 2005. For a full account of the battle at Binh Ba, see Gary McKay and Graeme Nicholas, *Jungle Tracks—Australian Armour in Viet Nam*, Allen & Unwin, Sydney, 2001.

39 The aviators were Captain Barry Donald and Second Lieutenant Alan Jellie, flying a Pilatus Porter at night and shot down on 3 December 1969.

40 Interview with Fred Pfitzner, Vung Tau, SRV, 8 October 2005

41 A military demarcation line on the 17th Parallel split Viet Nam as a result of the Geneva Accords, which came into effect at midnight on 22 July 1954.

42 Interview with Fred Pfitzner, 11 October 2005

43 Interview with Wendy Greenhalgh, Vung Tau, SRV, 8 October 2005

Chapter 6 Long Tan: The Cross

1 Elizabeth Stewart, 'Return to Vietnam', Paper, University of Newcastle, 2005

2 Interview with Steve Campling, Ho Chi Minh City, SRV, 12 August 2002

3 Interview with Bob Hansford, Ho Chi Minh City, SRV, 12 August 2002

4 Interview with Gail Campling, Ho Chi Minh City, SRV, 12 August 2002

5 Letter, Gail Campling, 24 December 2005

6 Interview with Paul Greenhalgh, Canberra, ACT, 20 February 2005

7 For Buick's account of the battle, see Bob Buick and Gary McKay, *All Guts and No Glory—The Story of a Long Tan Warrior*, Allen & Unwin, Sydney, 2000.

8 Interview with Paul Greenhalgh, 20 February 2005

9 Interview with Ron Shambrook, Brisbane, Qld, 14 July 2005

10 Interview with Ted and Joy Heffernan, Hoi An, SRV, 11 October 2005

11 Interview with John Taske, Hoi An, SRV, 11 October 2005

12 Ibid

13 Ibid

14 Interview with Ben Morris, Hoi An, SRV, 12 October 2005

15 Interview with Fred Pfitzner, Hoi An, SRV, 11 October 2005

16 Ibid

17 Interview with Ron Shambrook, 14 July 2005

18 Ibid

19 Interview with Peter Rogers, Yaroomba, Qld, 12 December 2005

20 Interview with Ron Shambrook, Hoi An, SRV, 12 October 2005

21 Interview with Roger and Tina Wainwright, Hoi An, SRV, 11 October 2005

22 Interview with Tony, Doffy and Rupert White, Ho Chi Minh City, SRV, 9 October 2005

23 Interview with Peter Isaacs, Hoi An, SRV, 11 October 2005

24 *Ba Ria–Vung Tau Guidebook*, 2005, and letter from Garry Adams, 23 November 2006

25 Interview with Bill Kromwyk, Mt Gravatt, Qld, 27 February 2006

26 Excerpt from *Wartime*, Issue 35, July 2006, p. 16

Chapter 7 The gamut of emotions

1 Interview with Garry Adams, Hoi An, SRV, 12 October 2005

2 Interview with Ron Shambrook, Hoi An, SRV, 12 October 2005

3 Interview with Garry Adams, 12 October 2005

4 Ibid

5 Letter, Steve Campling, 24 December 2005

6 Interview with Ted and Joy Heffernan, Hoi An, SRV, 11 October 2005

7   Ibid
8   Interview with Ron Shambrook, 12 October 2005
9   Interview with Ben Morris, Hoi An, SRV, 12 October 2005
10 Ibid
11 Interview with Peter Isaacs, Hoi An, SRV, 11 October 2005
12 Interview with John Taske, Hoi An, SRV, 11 October 2005
13 Interview with Tony, Doffy and Rupert White, Ho Chi Minh City, SRV, 9 October 2005
14 Interview with Paul and Wendy Greenhalgh, Hoi An, SRV, 12 October 2005
15 There are 24 Viet Nam servicemen buried in the Australian section of the War Cemetery at Terendak in Western Malaysia, and one (Warrant Officer Class 2 Conway) interred at Kranji Military Cemetery in Singapore.
16 Interview with Ben Morris, 12 October 2005
17 Ibid
18 Interview with Roger and Tina Wainwright, Hoi An, SRV, 11 October 2005
19 Ibid
20 Ibid
21 Interview with the White family, 9 October 2005
22 Letter, Bob Hann, 25 July 2006
23 Ibid
24 Letter, Garry Heskett, 19 June 2006
25 Interview with Peter Isaacs, 11 October 2005
26 Ibid
27 Ibid
28 Ibid
29 Letter, Peter Isaacs, 18 November 2005
30 Interview with Bill Kromwyk, Mt Gravatt, Qld, 27 February 2006
31 Ibid
32 Interview with John Taske, 11 October 2005
33 Ibid

34 Interview with Ron Shambrook, 12 October 2005

35 Letter, Ian Ryan, 2 May 2006

36 Ibid

37 Interview with Garry Adams, 12 October 2005

38 Ibid

39 Letter, Gail Campling, 24 December 2005

40 Interview with Paul and Wendy Greenhalgh, 12 October 2005

41 Interview with Garry Adams, 12 October 2005

42 Letter, Derrill De Heer, 17 May 2006

43 Ibid

44 Interview with Robyn Nolan, Coolum Beach, Qld, 3 May 2006

45 Ibid

46 Ibid

47 Ibid

48 Ibid

49 Ibid

50 Ibid

51 Ibid

52 Ibid

53 The War Atrocities Museum, as it was called when the report
    was written, is now known as the War Remnants Museum. It is
    located in the former US Ambassador's residence in Ho Chi
    Minh City and contains graphic displays showing images after
    the My Lai massacre, summary executions and many dead
    Vietnamese, as well as glass jars containing grotesque, seriously
    malformed unborn foetuses, claiming Agent Orange to be the
    cause. Regardless, there are no reports or images of Viet Cong
    or NVA atrocities, such as the massacre in Hué during the 1968
    Tet Offensive.

54 Interview with Robyn Nolan, 3 May 2006

55 Ibid

56 Ibid

57 Ibid

58 Ibid

59 Ibid

60 The VVCS is now known as the Veterans and Veterans Families Counselling Service and caters for all veterans of all conflicts.

61 Interview with Robyn Nolan, 3 May 2006

Chapter 8 Reflections

1 Interview with Paul and Wendy Greenhalgh, Hoi An, SRV, 12 October 2005

2 Ibid

3 Interview with Ted and Joy Heffernan, Hoi An, SRV, 11 October 2005

4 Ibid

5 Ibid

6 The Hippocratic Oath traditionally taken by physicians pertains to the ethical practice of medicine. It is widely believed that the oath was written by Hippocrates, the father of medicine, in the 4th century B.C.E., or by one of his students.

7 Interview with Ted and Joy Heffernan, 11 October 2005

8 Ibid

9 Interview with Peter Isaacs, Hoi An, SRV, 11 October 2005

10 Ibid

11 Interview with Ben Morris, Hoi An, SRV, 12 October 2005

12 Ibid

13 Interview with Fred Pfitzner, Hoi An, SRV, 11 October 2005

14 Ibid

15 Interview with Ron Shambrook, Hoi An, SRV, 12 October 2005

16 Interview with John Taske, Hoi An, SRV, 11 October 2005

17 Ibid

18 Interview with Roger and Tina Wainwright, Hoi An, SRV, 11 October 2005

19 Ibid

20 Interview with Tony, Doffy and Rupert White, Ho Chi Minh City, SRV, 9 October 2005
21 Ibid
22 Ibid
23 Interview with Ted and Joy Heffernan, 11 October 2005
24 Ibid
25 Interview with Roger and Tina Wainwright, 11 October 2005
26 Ibid
27 Interview with Tina Taske, Ho Chi Minh City, SRV, 9 October 2005
28 Ibid
29 Ibid
30 Ibid
31 Interview with Paul and Wendy Greenhalgh, 12 October 2005
32 Ibid
33 Interview with the White family, 9 October 2005
34 Interview with Doffy White, Vung Tau, SRV, 8 October 2005
35 Interview with the White family, 9 October 2005
36 Ibid
37 Ibid
38 Ibid
39 Ibid
40 Ibid
41 Letter, Kelly McKay, 7 December 2006

Epilogue

1 Interview with Garry Adams, Hoi An, SRV, 12 October 2005
2 Elizabeth Stewart, 'Return to Vietnam', Paper, University of Newcastle, 2005
3 I was present on this visit to Nui Dat on 17 August 1996.
4 I introduced Jim Richmond to Mr Sinh, a Long Tan veteran, on 17 August 1996.
5 Elizabeth Stewart, 'Return to Vietnam'

BIBLIOGRAPHY

Books

American Psychiatric Association, *Diagnostic and Statistical Manual of Mental Disorders*, 4th edn, American Psychiatric Association, Washington, DC, 2000

Buick, Bob and McKay, Gary, *All Guts & No Glory—The Story of a Long Tan Warrior*, Allen & Unwin, Sydney, 2000

Davies, Bruce and McKay, Gary, *The Men Who Persevered—The AATTV: The Most Decorated Australian Unit in the Viet Nam War*, Allen & Unwin, Sydney, 2005

Horner, David, *Duty First*, Allen & Unwin, Sydney, 1990

Karnow, Stanley, *Vietnam—A History, The First Complete Account of Vietnam at War*, Century Publishing, London, 1983

Mason, Florence and Storey, Robert, *Lonely Planet Vietnam, From Ho Chi Minh to the Honda Dream*, Lonely Planet Publications, Melbourne, 1991

McAulay, Lex, *The Battle of Coral, Fire Support Bases Coral and Balmoral May 1968*, Hutchinson, Melbourne, 1988

McKay, Gary, *Australia's Battlefields in Viet Nam, A Traveller's Guide*, Allen & Unwin, Sydney, 2004

——*Bullets, Beans and Bandages: Australians at War in Viet Nam*, Allen & Unwin, Sydney, 1999

——*Delta Four—Australian Riflemen in Vietnam*, Allen & Unwin, Sydney, 1996

——*In Good Company*, Allen & Unwin, Sydney, 1987

McKay, Gary and Nicholas, Graeme, *Jungle Tracks—Australian Armour in Viet Nam*, Allen & Unwin, Sydney, 2001

McNeill, Ian, *The Team: Australian Army Advisers in Vietnam 1962–1972*, Australian War Memorial, Canberra, 1984

Nolan, Keith William, *Battle For Hue, Tet 1968*, Presidio Press, California, 1983

O'Neill, Robert, *Vietnam Task: The 5th Battalion, The Royal Australian Regiment, 1966–67*, Cassell Australia, Melbourne, 1968

Prisor, Robert, *The End of The Line: The Siege at Khe Sanh*, W.W. Norton, New York, 1982

Yanagihara, Wendy and Ray, Nick, *Vietnam*, Lonely Planet, Melbourne, 2005

Papers

Stewart, Elizabeth, 'Return to Vietnam', a paper presented at the University of Newcastle conference 'The Vietnam War, Thirty Years On: Memories, Legacies, and Echoes', Newcastle, April 2005

Interviews

Adams, Garry, Hoi An, SRV, 12 October 2005

Campling, Gail and Steve, Ho Chi Minh City, SRV, 12 August 2002

Greenhalgh, Paul, Canberra, ACT, 20 February 2005

Greenhalgh, Paul and Wendy, Hoi An, SRV, 12 October 2005

Greenhalgh, Wendy, Vung Tau, SRV, 8 October 2005

Hansford, Bob, Ho Chi Minh City, SRV, 12 August 2002

Heffernan, Ted and Joy, Hoi An, SRV, 11 October 2005

Heskett, Garry, Bringelly, NSW, 15 May 1993
Isaacs, Peter, Hoi An, SRV, 11 October 2005
Kromwyk, Bill, Mt Gravatt, Qld, 27 February 2006
Morris, Ben, Hoi An, SRV, 12 October 2005
Morris, Ben, Yaroomba, Qld, 8 March 2005
Nolan, Robyn, Coolum Beach, Qld, 3 May 2006
Pfitzner, Fred, Hoi An, SRV, 11 October 2005
Pfitzner, Fred, Royalla, NSW, 2 September 2005
Pfitzner, Fred, Vung Tau, SRV, 8 October 2005
Rogers, Peter, Yaroomba, Qld, 23 May 2001 and 12 December 2005
Shambrook, Ron, Brisbane, Qld, 14 July 2005
Shambrook, Ron, Hoi An, SRV, 12 October 2005
Taske, John, Hoi An, SRV, 11 October 2005
Taske, Tina, Ho Chi Minh City, SRV, 9 October 2005
Wainwright, Roger, Canberra, ACT, 15 February 2005
Wainwright, Roger and Tina, Hoi An, SRV, 11 October 2005
White, Doffy, Vung Tau, SRV, 8 October 2005
White, Rupert, Vung Tau, SRV, 8 October 2005
White, Tony, Doffy and Rupert, Ho Chi Minh City, SRV, 9 October
    2005

Letters

Adams, Garry, 23 November 2006
Campling, Gail, 24 December 2005
Campling, Steve, 24 December 2005
De Heer, Derrill, 17 May 2006
Hann, Bob, 25 July 2006
Heffernan, Ted, 18 September 2005
Heskett, Garry, 19 June 2006
Heskett, Suzanne, 16 June 2006

Isaacs, Peter, 7 September 2005
Isaacs, Peter, 18 November 2005
McKay, Kelly, 7 December 2006
Nolan, Robyn, 2 May 2006
Rogers, Peter, 24 March 2005
Ryan, Ian, 2 May 2006
Taske, John, 13 September 2005
White, Tony, 9 September 2005

INDEX